Utopia, community care
and the retreat
from the asylums

Utopia, community care and the retreat from the asylums

Dylan Ronald Tomlinson

Open University Press
Milton Keynes · Philadelphia

Open University Press
Celtic Court
22 Ballmoor
Buckingham
MK18 1WX

and

1900 Frost Road, Suite 101
Bristol, PA 19007, USA

First Published 1991

British Library Cataloguing-in-Publication Data

Utopia, community care and the retreat from the
asylums.
  I. Tomlinson, Dylan
  362.20941

  ISBN 0-335-09623-9
  ISBN 0-335-09622-0 pbk

Library of Congress Cataloging-in-Publication Data

Tomlinson, Dylan Ronald, 1955–
    Utopia, community care, and the retreat from the asylums/Dylan
  Ronald Tomlinson.
      p.   cm.
    Includes bibliographical references and index.
    ISBN 0-335-09623-9 (hb)   ISBN 0-335-09622-0 (pb)
    1. Psychiatric hospitals – England – London – History – 20th century.
  2. Hospital closures – England – London – History – 20th century.
  3. Psychiatric hospital patients – England – London – History – 20th
  century.   4. Community mental health services – England – London –
  History – 20th century.   I. Title.
  RC450.G7T66   1991
  362.2′1′0942109048 – dc20   91-22585 CIP

Typeset by Inforum Typesetting, Portsmouth
Printed in Great Britain by Biddles Ltd, Guildford and King's Lynn

To Laurie

Contents

Acknowledgements

No one person is an island and books are not created by individuals. Innumerable people have influenced the development of my work. But I am particularly grateful for the unfailing support of my colleagues in the Team for Assessment of Psychiatric Services: Dr John Carrier, Mrs Rowena Kendal, Professor Julian Leff and Mrs Margaret Wallace.

I would also like to express my thanks to the officers of the North East Thames Regional Health Authority, who allowed an unfettered academic independence to flourish in this study.

Dr Bernard Heine gave me kind encouragement during the difficult period in which I was endeavouring to establish the fieldwork. Dr Cathie O'Driscoll generously allowed me to consult her own collection of literature on deinstitutionalization programmes. My friend and colleague Paul Watt made invaluable comments on a draft of the manuscript. Equally, my father, William Tomlinson, made a significant improvement of it possible by a zealous proofreading.

Finally I wish to thank Mr Patrick Davis of the London School of Economics' Publications Committee and the two anonymous referees who read an earlier draft of Chapters 4 to 6, whose comments helped me to reshape the work into book form.

Due to the nature of the material some quotations have not been referenced.

Abbreviations

AHA	area health authority
CHC	community health council
CMHC	community mental health centre
DGH	district general hospital
DGM	district general manager
DHA	district health authority
DHSS	Department of Health and Social Security
DMO	district medical officer
DMT	district management team
GP	general practitioner
HAS	Health Advisory Service
HLM	Habitations Loyer à Modéré
IHA	Islington Health Authority
ILEA	Inner London Education Authority
JCPT	joint care planning team
LBH	London Borough of Haringey
LBI	London Borough of Islington
LBWF	London Borough of Waltham Forest
NETRHA	North East Thames Regional Health Authority
NHS	National Health Service
NMH	North Middlesex Hospital (Edmonton)
NSF	National Schizophrenia Fellowship (Surbiton)
PRA	Psychiatric Rehabilitation Association
RAWP	Resource Allocation Working Party
RHA	regional health authority
RMO	regional medical officer
RNO	regional nursing officer
RNP	regional nurse planner
RTO	regional team of officers

TAPS	Team for Assessment of Psychiatric Services
UCH	University College Hospital (Bloomsbury)
UGM	unit general manager

Introduction

A new utopia is enchanting society. Resting on a cult of localism and a rejection of fixed term representative forms of authority, it can be called an athenian utopia. Within it autonomous individuals requiring education, health or other welfare services invite tenders for their supply from third parties. A benign state watches over the subsequent contracting process of decision and provision.

Current European debates on deinstitutionalization, decentralization and deregulation show evidence of a belief that this utopia is achievable. A wide-ranging movement away from state provision of welfare services is underway. Two principal forces have been at work in this movement. The first is dissatisfaction with the cost-ineffectiveness and under-achievement of centralized social planning. Poverty has not been eradicated: the health of people belonging to the working class remains significantly worse than that of those in the middle and upper classes. The second is the need to restrain growth in public expenditure on welfare. Despite the best efforts of governments committed to liberalism and self-reliance, spending on welfare has not decreased in real terms.

In Britain, significant restriction of the post-war growth of social services began under the Wilson government of the 1960s. A perceived fiscal crisis in the decade which followed prompted examination of some of the more fundamental assumptions of municipal planning and provision. By 1990 many European governments had devised programmes for shifting provision to the private and voluntary sectors, following the principle that consumers should be able to choose between entrepreneurs charging for their services. Cash benefits would support such choices.

Into this larger evolution of welfare was pitched the programme for the rundown of the English mental hospitals, put forward as a novel process around the end of the 1970s.

In taking the decision to close one such hospital (Claybury) and part of another (Friern) by transferring patients to community placements, the North East Thames Regional Health Authority (NETRHA) committed it- self to monitor and evaluate the effects of what was seen as a novel reset- tlement process. Three research programmes were set up: a 'clinical' evaluation of the outcome for each long-stay patient of transfer to the community, an economic appraisal of the costs of the new services in comparison with those of the hospitals, and a study of the policy-making process through which these services were to be devised and locally imple- mented. These three programmes constituted a unique longitudinal eval- uation of mental hospital closures. For the purpose of undertaking them, the Team for Assessment of Psychiatric Services (TAPS) was formed in 1985. The opportunity was thereby created for studying a test case of the contraction and contracting reforms which the NHS and local government had been subject to in the 1970s and 1980s. In order to achieve closures, health authorities were given powers to purchase care for their clients from outside agencies. Central government also allowed considerable discretion to the authorities in their devising of alternatives to the mental hospitals. There was thus ample scope for local entrepreneurial responses and nego- tiations. Technical assessment was to be a cornerstone of closure, ranging from estimates of likely rates of patient deaths and discharges, through scoring the potential for rehabilitation of hospital residents, to evaluating the public health needs of local populations.

It was these elements which were to fall under the scrutiny of the deci- sion making research, to develop which, NETRHA's officers took aca- demic advice. Dr John Carrier of the London School of Economics drew up a protocol within which were proposed the following terms of reference for the principal researcher:

1 to 'work with' officers and 'be at' meetings concerned with decisions of change
2 to steep him/herself in the process of decision-making while retaining sufficient objectivity to be able to highlight key participants, events and values
3 to document changes in opinion, significant events, local political climates and central government's impact on decision-making
4 to write interim papers, for discussion by participants of the research interpretation of events.

As research sociologist, and first officer appointed to TAPS, the author has carried out this policy making study, the results from which are presented in Chapters 4 to 6.

Empirical analysis of the implementation of state policy tends to have had three foci: organizational processes, structural explanations and action research.[1] The organizational analysts have been concerned with the polar opposition between rational planning and incrementalism, and with the relative inputs of central and local agencies to the intended outcomes of policy. Structuralists have been more interested in the economic and political forces shaping the state's activity. Fiscal constraint, populist rejection of state bureaucracy, trade union influences, post-Fordism in capitalist techniques of production, and ideological control by the state are their stock in trade. Action researchers on the other hand are interested in facilitating change and problem-solving within the agencies where they do their work. Often following the tradition of London's Tavistock clinic in this country, they seek to give participants greater insight into the decision-making forces and processes. By understanding the psychology of the process that has produced company or organizational conflicts, participants can devise their own policy solutions.

The approach adopted in this book is one in which organizational issues are underpinned by an understanding of structural influences. I am particularly concerned with the place of the state within community, because of the implications for this relationship which the devolution of mental health services from large, remote, impersonal institutions, holds. The theoretical framework which results from this treatment of the empirical issues is set out in Chapter 2.

As the terms of reference show, a clear choice of participant observation as a method of study was made at an early stage, to be supplemented by interviews with decision-makers. During the initial period of attendance at planning team meetings it became clear to me that a small number of 'key informants' offered the most insightful and knowledgeable advice about decisions and their origins. The method I adopted of making use of such informants was thus similar in this sense to that of W. F. Whyte in his famous study of 'street corner society'.[2] In like manner to his key informants, my own would often say, 'You should have been there when such and such happened'. Whyte felt that he made one mistake in becoming involved in a local campaign. Mindful of this I have been careful not to be drawn into any local campaigns during the research and to keep the method located at the 'observer-as-participant' end of the spectrum and away from the 'participant-as-observer' end.

Completing this study has been part of a personal journey. In 1982 I worked for the first time in a mental hospital as a nursing auxiliary. This is work commonly undertaken by graduates interested in a career in the helping professions. But I had deeper concerns being, like many others, closely involved in informal care-giving.

After listening to and analysing the debates about the practical acts of deinstitutionalization as a researcher for more than five years, I began to feel uncertain about my own views on the various philosophies propounded by planners and their critics. In order to clear certain doubts in my mind I went to work for a period in a hospital outside the North East Thames Region, again as an auxiliary, on a part-time basis. This experience settled my own views on the options in mental health then being canvassed within planning bodies which I observed, and gave a focus to the conclusions of this book.

Chapter 1 sets the European and American scene of mental hospital rundown. In Chapter 2 the theoretical framework is introduced. In Chapter 3 I describe the bare bones of the closure processes for the first big asylums in England to close, namely those at Powick in Worcestershire, Banstead in Surrey, and Exminster in Devon. These English hospitals are singled out because vigorous closure initiatives on this scale were not adopted before 1982 in Scotland or Ireland, while in Wales developments were at a more formative stage.

Chapters 4 to 6 present the empirical material from the Friern and Claybury study. Description of the planning processes is followed by discussion of clients' own views of the outcome and of the 'verdicts' on it which were reached by the professional researchers and lay bodies involved.

In the conclusion, I propose a number of strategies for solving the planning problems of the rundown of asylums and for achieving community ownership of dehospitalization programmes.

References

1 Glennerster, H., Korman, N., Marslen-Wilson, F. and Meredith, B. (1982). *Social Planning*, London, London School of Economics.
2 Whyte, W.F. (1943). *Street Corner Society*, Chicago, Ill., University of Chicago Press.

1

The American and European context of reform

The United States of America

Deinstitutionalization in Europe and the United States of America is a process that is still very much unfolding. No country has managed to do away entirely with reliance on state psychiatric hospitals. Even in the USA, where a radical process of resettlement got underway at an early stage, most reported episodes of mental illness are still treated at these institutions. Indeed the rate of admissions to state hospitals in the mid-1970s was double that of the 1950s.[1]

However, the increased rate at which new patients are admitted has clearly been more than matched by the rate at which patients have been discharged. The massive decline of the state hospital population in the USA, from a peak of half a million in 1955 to 191,000 twenty years later, indicates that the scale of change is indeed highly significant, and that, in some form, a transfer of care has occurred.[2]

Many observers suggest that this transfer has had mainly adverse effects on the population concerned. On her own examination of the evidence, Bachrach has argued that community services have not generally assisted the chronic population and that communities differ in the degree to which they have been 'ready' to accept the retreat from institutions.[3] Kirk and Therrien, commenting on the reduction of the hospital population in Hawaii, identify a 'myth of rehabilitation'. The myth involves two elements of wishful thinking. The first is that the removal of institutional conditions is in itself a therapeutic act. The second is that staff who transfer from hospitals to the community change their attitudes toward their charges, taking on new enabling and nurturing rather than rule-enforcing and limit-setting care roles.[4]

By the 1980s the phenomenon of transinstitutionalization had been uncovered by Lamb and Brown amongst others.[5] This involved a straightforward transfer of patients from mental hospitals to board-with-care houses or nursing homes. These moves were condemned on the grounds that backward conditions in hospital were being exchanged for backward conditions in the community. Such an intention had not been apparent in the earlier government policy of the 1960s. An impressive result of the policy was the creation of 507 fully functioning community mental health centres (CMHCs) by mid-1975. The centres were designed to provide 'a coordinated program of at least five essential mental health services: in-patient services, emergency services, partial hospitalization (such as day care), out patients services, and consultation and education services'.[6] Charged with the task of treatment and prevention and after care, they seem to have failed to develop an effective community support system for discharged patients. Administrative problems played their part in this story since the centres were not run by the same authorities as those managing the state hospitals. 'Moreover in the rush to reduce their census the hospitals discharged patients long before most of the community centres had been established and before supporting programmes had been developed.'[7]

Underlying the mental health movement in the USA was 'widespread faith in the ability of mental health experts to effectively manipulate the social environment'. Among professionals there was a belief that 'perhaps two-thirds of the population were psychiatrically ill', which meant that there was 'a gigantic opportunity for human progress'.[8] But the centres which were the linchpin of the movement were criticized both for erring too much on the side of prevention – tackling such issues as racism, poverty and education in the communities served, and for doing too little prevention, this arising from the affiliation of most of them to general and mental hospitals. The attempt to adopt a public health model, bringing a whole host of welfare agencies to primary intervention opened up 'a power struggle from which the mental health field had yet to recover', according to Gardner (writing in 1977).[9]

Aside from those who were involved in intellectual and political movements it was an open question how far mental health experts would be received into the bosom of the target population. Many potential customers might feel more comfortable where agencies were not aiming at supervision of their minds. If the help available was to be a free good then, in the USA, there would be a considerable amount of stigma attached to recipients of it.

If it were to be successful the mental health movement would have to move away from any strong association with welfare. The mental health centres, from which so much was expected for the future, were designed to become self-funding from fees and diverse agency support. The federal pump-priming for their establishment, eventually extended to cover their first eight years, was not intended to support them for the long term. This strategy neglected the fact that most users of such services in the USA were poor by definition, since the more well-to-do would elect to go to private practitioners. It was highly unlikely that the chronic population discharged from the mental hospitals would provide an affluent enough target population to support self-funding mental health centres. This policy assumption seems to have been naive, and to have been built on the extravagantly high hopes of the public health model of intervention.

Italy

The initial impressions of the Italian reform of 1978 suggested a similarly disappointing outcome to that in the USA.[10] However, there is a dearth of systematic research into the changes effected. Bollini and Mollica contend that early reports of catastrophic results were often based upon 'short visits and superficial knowledge of the Italian mental health care system'.[11] More recent reviews suggest that the government prohibition of admissions to mental hospitals has, at least partially, succeeded in achieving the development of community services.

There are of course significant political differences between the USA and Italy, even though both come under the rubric of industrial capitalism. Trade unions and the socialist movement have traditionally been weak in the USA, while Labour or Social Democratic parties have dominated some European governments, depending on a strong undercurrent of what has been called 'Eurocommunism'. In Italy local communist control of municipal affairs, particularly in the north, is well established. As health services are run by elected authorities, there is much scope for 'municipal socialism' in the administration of mental health. As Ramon comments,

> Marxist views are not approached as merely theoretical formulations but also as guidelines for action. For example, the emphasis in the organisational framework on power sharing among the different professional disciplines involved, on not making redundant any workers, and the focus on the lay community demonstrate the impact of Italian Marxist thinking on the reform group.[12]

It is often suggested that in Italy the general public is more receptive to the idea of mental hospital residents returning to live in the community. The belief in collective action for change was mentioned earlier. In this context the development of co-operatives is a notable feature of the reform. By means of the co-operatives patients who had previously been subject to institutional peonage – payment of token wages in exchange for hospital work – have been able to earn wages comparable with those in the wider economy. An example is given in the review of the Italian reform edited by Perris and Kemali.[13] This initiative was taken in Trieste in 1973, when all patients who had undergone 'ergotherapy' in the hospital combined together as a co-operative to carry out cooking, ward work, cleaning and maintenance tasks. 'At the end of a month-long dispute they succeeded in obtaining the contract for these jobs from the hospital administration and were consequently entitled to the wage guaranteed by the National Cleaners Contract.'[14] The co-operative, made up of both former patients and ordinary workers, continued to hold the contract for cleaning all mental health centres and former hospital buildings after the closure of the hospital.

Much has also been made of the catharsis for the 'community' of the exodus. Again in the case of Trieste, Dell'Aqua describes how patients, painters, doctors, nurses and students built a blue horse – the Marco Cavallo – which led a joyful procession of about 6,000 patients through the town, and on to a celebration of the emptying of the first ward, held at a local primary school.

> The coming out of the horse, following long discussions and meetings between doctors, nurses, patients and artists, was also an opportunity to denounce the miserable conditions of the Mental Hospital, the backwardness of the law in force, the nurses' working conditions and, above all, the lack of real prospects for all those patients who were already capable of living outside the hospital.[15]

Ramon considers that there were in fact similar political obstacles to the achievement of mental hospital closures in Italy as have been found in Britain. The majority of the psychiatric profession's members were not in favour of the reform. There was no evidence for the feasibility of such change. The ruling coalition in Parliament in 1978 was opposed to the reform. The law was passed 'more by default than by intention'. Much was owed to the small Radical party, which collected the necessary 500,000 signatures to obtain a referendum on the issue. To avoid the possible political embarrassment of such a referendum, the government preferred to make the law itself.

Four 'change-facilitating factors' are picked out by Ramon; heavy and unchanging reliance on segregated institutions; the existence of a minority of psychiatrists prepared to act politically (while not having the desire to act in a party political framework); the autonomous nature of the regions leading to more enthusiastic reform beginning in socialist and communist areas; and perhaps most importantly for the concerns of this book,

> The wide acceptance of the positive value of collective action, typical of Italy for a long time [which] meant a well-established tradition existed for mobilising community support.[16]

This social environment for devolution contrasts strongly with that in the USA. This is evident from an analysis of public opinion on welfare in the USA in comparison with opinion in other countries. Shapiro and Young for example found that Americans are consistently less supportive of state intervention than are the people of other industrial countries, if not always markedly so.[17] They ascribe the difference to the fact that Americans value equality of opportunity rather than equality of outcome. While attitudes on education and medical care strongly support either direct state provision or state guidance and support for private provision, attitudes on income support and urban relief are much more mixed.

In contrast to all other social welfare policies, public assistance programmes for the poor are the most controversial. These policies remind many Americans of deadbeats, fraud and entangled bureaucracies; and they appear to provide serious disincentives for employment. As is well known, Americans are uneasy toward the terms 'welfare' or relief in contrast to 'assistance for the poor' or similar phrases.[18]

Thus Americans are found to prefer distribution of food stamps rather than broader policies for a guaranteed minimum income. Their views on programmes for urban renewal tend to follow similar lines to their views on welfare, with large-scale intervention not seen as a public responsibility.

These differences between American and European views have ominous implications for deinstitutionalization since, as already pointed out, many chronic patients are poor. There is also evidence that they drift into the urban areas which are the subject of decay.[19]

Marmor also comments that

America's ethos of limited, constrained government remains the accepted rhetoric. The nation has a very large civil service but a mixture of disdain for and suspicion of its civil servants . . . our leading governmental institutions are without the benefits of great formal authority and respect. American society fragments into the complicated pressure groups and local constituencies. But the American polity remains rooted in a cast of mind appropriate to a commercial agrarian society, requiring the most minimalist of government performance.[20]

This view fits with those of the political scientists, Lindblom and Benson. They see the output of state policies in the USA as the result of interagency negotiation, rather than central or local direction. Direction of social policy from the centre is rarely promised or achieved. Policy tends to be incremental in outcome. This suggests that the major transfer of care from state hospitals has taken place without any specific political driving force. Fiscal crisis, however, has been as apparent in the USA as in Europe. States were therefore keen to see the federally supported mental health centres as the new agencies which could play the leading role.

Though there has been a clear public responsibility for the long-term residents of mental hospitals, public responsibility for those discharged has not been so well established. For many years Medicaid did not finance mental health care for adults, while Marmor comments that the amount of benefits for care outside hospital that was made available totalled a 'derisory' $250 per year in 1987. Though there might be public support for better insurance programmes, if somewhat thin, because of the stagflation-induced social policy crisis, there was no 'mass attention, supportive sentiment, or a willingness of governmental actors to place mental health finance prominently on the agenda'.

A final element in the USA is the legal interest in mental health which focuses strongly on the individual and the right not to be committed except in extreme circumstances. The corollary of such a concern with the individual is a lack of concern with the collectivity.

> What had once been a largely invisible world of mental hospitals, private suffering, and professional services now appears in local communities as homelessness, strange persons in public, and bewilderment about who is responsible for whom. In such a context no wonder that those preoccupied with the mentally ill feel so frustrated with the politics of fiscal restraint in all the industrial democracies.[21]

In one sense this is comforting for the concerned public in Britain, since visions of an apocalypse for those discharged seem less credible given the differences in approaches to welfare. But the American approach to community care does not necessarily diverge from that of Europe where the response of state agencies to public opinion is concerned. Atherton argues that the mass of the American people remain committed to support for the 'genuinely poor, sick, disabled and disadvantaged', but not to a redistributive welfare programme.[22]

The wider European context

Since the radical reform could happen in the uncollectivist and weakly welfarist USA as well as in the collectivist and welfarist Italy, the obvious question to ask is why it didn't happen elsewhere in Europe.

Many obstacles appear to stem from central–local relations and conflict between the public and private sector. Municipal autonomy in the regions of Italy and state autonomy in the USA seems to go some way to account for the ease of transfer of care. This appears to be confirmed by current trends in Spain, where the development of autonomous regions encompassing health and social care is leading to a strong administrative reform which has, as one of its central objectives, the establishment of primary care services for people suffering from mental illness.[23] By contrast, in Greece, which is divided up into nine health administration districts, little reform has taken place. This is despite the passing of a law in 1981 providing for many of the Italian reform components: general hospital wards, community mental health centres and procedures for linking the various sectors. The system of health district administration does not lend itself to local initiatives, since the districts do not relate to any natural geographic catchment areas. By 1987 five inpatient units in general hospitals had been created and thirteen mental health centres. But there had been only a small decrease in mental hospital beds and little sign of a significant shift to different forms of care.[24]

Portugal provides an interesting case study of administrative problems. In 1981 co-operation with the Swedish government produced a programme for health care which provided a stimulus for reform of the asylums. Planning proposals for a new system of mental health services for the areas of Lisbon and Oporto were developed. According to Ribeiro, these proposals took their principles from the French system of psychiatric sectors linking hospitals and after care.[25] A community psychiatry system was adopted which had the mental health centre at the middle. In a short and irreverent sketch which aims to explain subsequent inaction on implementing the reform in Portugal, Ribeiro calls on a concept in the Portuguese language known as *desenrasca* – multiform resistance to rational planning and change. The resistance has eight aspects to it:

1 informal rejection or acceptance of the planning proposal, without expressing it at a formal level
2 kill it using silence
3 personalization of the planning proposal
4 cosmetic reformulation of mental health policies, objectives and action programmes and recommendations
5 internalization of planning proposals without reference to them
6 hidden criticisms that only appear in the interpersonal context: the classic 'utopian plan', 'not feasible', 'without economic basis'
7 avoiding of confrontation
8 and last but not least the complete inability of presenting different alternatives.

Ribeiro's argument points to the significance of distinguishing the universal approbation accorded to community care policies from political initiatives for their implementation. While most European countries have developed new forms of service, there appears to be a silent majority vote for the retention of the mental hospitals.

This scenario seems to apply to the position in The Netherlands, otherwise seen as being in the forefront of community care. Although there was a reduction in mental hospital beds of 17 per cent between 1955 and 1975, this hardly bears comparison with the trend in the USA where for the corresponding period the reduction was 66 per cent.[26] Since 1985 there has been only a marginal reduction in mental hospital beds: 'I think we lost some somewhere', as Dr Peter Verbraak, Director of de Grote Bek Hospital in Groningen, recently commented.[27]

Yet reform in The Netherlands began early, in the 1930s, with the avoidance of hospital admissions. According to van der Grinten, this trend originally arose because of the effects of the trade recession of the period on the municipal authorities funding patient care in the large hospitals.[28]

'Extramural care' was seen as a means of reducing this burden. In Amsterdam, Querido introduced a twenty-four-hour domiciliary support system, linked with the care of general practitioners. This system was also adopted in other large cities. A number of different types of psychiatric crisis intervention services had become available by the 1980s. These included

> eight general crisis centres, with or without beds, alternative psychosocial centres based largely on religious principles, specialized services for youngsters, outreaching services as part of community mental health centres and emergency room services as part of the general hospitals.[29]

With the 'relatively dense network of outpatient and day patient services which exist in the country', it is surprising that the radicalism of Italy has not been contagious.

In fact the Dutch face some of the same administrative problems in achieving change that beset other European countries, principally in the lack of a system for municipal co-ordination. Many of the large hospitals are controlled by religious foundations, with the government role being largely limited to funding patient care through insurance schemes. The services of the hospitals have only recently become more integrated with primary care services outside. Previously the hospitals tended to be in competition for clients and resources with rehabilitation and primary care agencies.

The religious/municipal dichotomy, coupled with a lack of direct state provison of health services, probably accounts for the lack of a widespread deinstitutionalizing or care transfer movement. The insurers have also been reluctant to underwrite non-medical forms of care outside the hospital sector. It is only recently that the municipal authorities and hospital boards have begun to discuss the possibility of changing the insurers' conditions of funding so that they are more permissive of non-medical intervention and support. But there are signs too that the professional care providers seek to halt the slight trend in reduction which has taken place in the role of the mental hospital. Thus Giel argues that

> While the Dutch government is actively planning to reduce the number of hospital beds, particularly those for long-stay patients, it takes little notice of the reality of mental health care in The Netherlands, cherishing various misconceptions regarding institutionalism and community care. [Drawing on a case register summary he continues] any further reduction of mental hospital beds will be to the detriment of the chronic mentally disturbed person.[30]

Perhaps the least change of all has occurred in France and the former Federal Republic of Germany (FRG). France is a country which led the therapeutic enterprise of building the asylums in the nineteeth century. Its Lunacy Act of 1838, which required every department to develop a public asylum, can be seen as a model for the legislation of other countries. But despite being subject to the second wave of pan-European reform in psychiatry since the 1940s, France has not moved away from the asylums with any speed.

Mangen and Castel relate an appalling tale of how the circumstances in which the French asylums found themselves in the Second World War prompted experiment with alternatives. Tens of thousands of mental hospital patients died from starvation in the hospitals. To attempt to save as many residents of one hospital as possible, two psychiatrists, aided by a group of resistance workers, engaged in a desperate effort to resettle them with households in the surrounding area where they could be fed. The patients 'were quickly integrated into the life of the small community and it was found that many of them were surviving better outside than inside the hospital'.[31]

One of the interesting facets of developments in France, which also applies to the situation in the former FRG, is that the legacy of mental hospitals is not seen as an intrinsically untenable one. They are not considered to be non-viable either on the grounds of their isolation and remoteness from the communities they serve, or on the grounds that they are physically falling into a state of dilapidation. In 1960 a new French programme for mental health services provided for hospitals to be converted on village plan lines. The objective was one of 'adaptation and humanisation, not mass closure'.[32] Nevertheless France possessed a technocratic system of sectorization across the whole country with departments and communes being mandated to provide local outpatient and prevention services. While government and insurance funds are available toward the cost of these services the provincial municipalities still have to contribute local funding for their development. Thus there has to be some degree of policy enthusiasm for prevention and outpatient services if the dominance of hospital inpatient beds over the care system is to change in any one administrative area.

Reliance on the nature of local commitment has been a considerable obstacle to lessening dependence on the mental hospitals. Mangen and Castel suggest that

> by the late Seventies it was generally acknowledged that a funding system partially dependent on the departments would be unlikely to assure speedy progress towards a comprehensive service in the sector and would do nothing to reduce the substantial regional inequalities in the distribution of extra hospital facilities.[33]

As in The Netherlands, the insurers have also resisted subsidizing treatment which is primarily non-medical, though they do fund 30 per cent of the *dispensaires* prevention programmes administered primarily within the local government system.

In the mid-1980s the French government did act to try to redress these trends, taking over responsibility for extra hospital services from the local departments. Plans were also made to phase out unoccupied mental hospital beds and to transfer others to community services. Nevertheless the key point about the lack of political interest in change is made tellingly by Mangen and Castel:

> Whatever the feeling inside psychiatry, mental health is not a major political issue in the country as a whole. The vote for the 1838 Act was preceded by impassioned debate in both parliamentary chambers and aroused widespread interest throughout France. That level of public and political interest has never been rekindled.[34]

Britain

The history of British policy has been discussed elsewhere in comprehensive terms.[35] Therefore it will not be dealt with in any detail here. The main focus of the discussion which follows is on the relative importance of administrative, economic and therapeutic factors in the evolution of policy.

Britain has been subject to the same decline in long-stay beds and has responded in the same way as other European countries to this fall in the mental hospital population. Plans were laid from the early 1960s for the development of non-asylum types of treatment. General hospital units would provide the typical destigmatizing, cure-centred approach being followed around the psychiatric globe. As these units were set up, they would replace the functions of the large hospitals, which would be required only for the care of the old long-stay patients, a cohort admitted before the outdoor mode of treatment was to become common and schizophrenia was thought uncontrollable in the community. Since they had become used to hospitals it was believed both unfair to them and impracticable in resettlement terms to ship them out to the community. As the cohort died out and were not replaced, the asylums could be shut down. But demographic trends would determine the rundown rate. As in other Western European countries north of Italy, there was to be no pre-emptive national closure policy. Government has stressed at several points that it seeks the development of local district services first, with asylums to close only when the latter services can cope with the patient workload.

This suggests that closures have not stemmed primarily from an objective of economic rationalization. Their rundown had more to do with their social function becoming anachronistic. The country was not ringing to calls for their shutdown from either legislators or the judiciary. There was no significant social movement for community medicine, or people's councils for health/social services or self-help. This perhaps reflected the endemic nationalism (rather than localism) of health and social welfare in Britain. The National Health Service (NHS) was always based on administrative units and had a non-elected board of control. Social services were provided by local councils but these councils were not especially noted for being bonded to local cultures.[36] Within these councils, social services were strictly regulated. In the 1970s and 1980s their work was dominated by statutory duties toward the care of children. While there were many attempts to devolve welfare services to a neighbourhood level, the overall decline in local authority power relative to the centre vitiated much of the potential for popular decision-making. At the same time community development failed as a 1970s movement to sustain the campaigning ability of local residents and their autonomy in civic affairs.[37]

As an organization for the administration of medicine, the NHS tended to interpret community care to mean the devolution of hospital-centred services into a 'primary care' catchment area.[38] The transfer of services in the asylums to the community fell in with this approach. The district general hospital (DGH) units carried through the first stage of devolution of services. Instead of relying on admissions to an asylum serving several district areas, each district would, in the DGH, have its own core treatment rooms. The second phase would be carried out by the dispersal of nurses and psychologists into general practice surgeries and day hospitals. Alternatively, free-standing mental health centres could offer outdoor treatment and support.

So, above all, the picture is of an administrative reform taking place for new mental health services to be created. Initially it was believed that the general devolution to smaller administrative entities would, in itself, create the conditions for asylums to be closed down. The hospitals more remote from their catchment area were thus the natural early candidates for closure.

Closures had implications beyond the NHS, however. The main problem was that if the new devolved NHS services were to replace the asylums' treatment, then a structure of long-term support would be needed for those who, albeit now being able to live in the community rather than vegetate as long-term inpatients, still mostly required structured day care or home visiting or occupation. This requirement, not being a treatment need, was not primarily an NHS responsibility. The asylums had of course long predated the bifurcation of health and welfare in the centralized system. With their dissolution the health and welfare functions would have to be distributed between the newer health and social services administrative entities. Local authorities, although not being party to the devolution of the NHS provision, would have to be asked to take upon themselves a serious long-term support role.

But there were, inevitably, in a period when municipal provision was subject to restraint, problems about the achievement of the social services support that would match the NHS devolution. Through joint planning forums, there was a mechanism for co-ordinating health and social care across the boundaries of the statutory sectors from 1974. The administrative situation in Britain was thus favourable to change. But much depended, as elsewhere in Europe, on the attitude of the municipal authorities towards committing resources for new services. Local authorities had a duty to assess those judged to be 'at risk' or 'vulnerable' and the state had to take responsibility for the supervision of care. Beyond that the White Paper Better Services for the Mentally Ill (1975) also set out rates of provision which health and local authorities *ought* to be aiming to achieve. For 'oughtness' could be read council discretion about what priorities they had for the distribution of 'new moneys'. These were, naturally under much pressure. If social services committees did exercise any clout over other committees within councils, the strong prior claim of children was already established.

In 1976 central government did take an initiative to try to influence local policy-making in favour of the long-stay dependent groups. By means of explicit priorities the centre aimed to manoeuvre the localities into promoting long-term clients up the league table of social care.[39] Within an annual 2 per cent growth in the budget for personal social services, and a 1.8 per cent growth in NHS revenue, services for elderly, mentally handicapped and mentally ill people would receive a proportionally greater allocation than the mainstream services for short-term consultation. But there were priorities within the priorities. Whereas 2.8 per cent growth was projected in services for mentally handicapped people, only 1.8 per cent growth was to be devoted to those who were mentally ill, the average across the health and welfare sector. The policy held out little prospect of significant change.

The *Care in the Community* initiative in 1981 attempted to force the pace. Through it, government addressed for the first time the issue of the long-stay population in all the institutions for elderly, mentally handicapped and mentally ill people. Subsequent guidance enabled regional health authorities (RHAs) to pay grants to local authorities for the support of people resettled in the community from the NHS hospitals. Somewhat cautiously the government hinted at fairly large-scale programmes of reintegration:

> Most people discharged from hospital psychiatric care have had only a short period as in patients and do not need long-term help after leaving. Other people have spent many years in hospital and could no longer live outside it. There *may*, however, be up to 5,000 people now in hospital who fall in between these two groups and *may* be capable of leading more independent lives. . . . There may also be scope for new approaches to the care of elderly severely mentally infirm people now in hospital.[40]

On one level this statement was not staking out any new policy, merely raising theoretical possibilities. On another level it signalled a new departure. The White Paper of 1975 mentioned above had simply referred to the virtual impracticability of asking social service departments to commit themselves to major investment in a programme for mentally ill people. In addition the important statement was made that

> In the last resort achievement will be dependent on the community's willingness to accept an increased responsibility for those of its members who are or have been mentally ill . . . time is needed to prepare the way and to accustom the community to these added responsibilities. The very length of the timescale may help in this respect.[41]

Against this pessimistic background, the *Care in the Community* optimism about the possibilities for long-stay patients to live more independently seemed to betoken a change of central thinking. Was this driven by the need to ship out the occupants of the decaying and unviable institutions?

The answer is that it is difficult to see a conspiracy theory at work. As early as 1968 the government recognized that the development of DGH treatment services was not leading to the replacement of asylums.[42] But on the other hand nothing was done about that beyond the statement of the obvious that there would be no votes for mental health within the welfare budget to fund alternative long-term community care to that given in institutions. Such funding would have to be clawed back from the contraction of the institutions. In 1977 in *The Way Forward*, it was stated that

> It is clearly undesirable and often more expensive to admit or keep in district general hospitals or long stay hospitals old or mentally ill or mentally handicapped people who could be properly looked after in the community. This will be avoided only if adequate progress can be made in developing community services including community hospitals . . . the release of really substantial resources for deployment in the development of local psychiatric services generally is likely to be achieved only with the closure of a whole hospital. Regions ought to be looking to the future and planning the replacement of major mental illness hospitals.[43]

It is possible to detect a slight warming-up of the issue between the late 1960s and the late 1970s, given these prompts for RHAs to think about taking some positive action. But as has been seen, if changes were to be brought about, they were to be initiated by making changes internally to NHS services. The question being asked was 'Could the old long-stay patients be moved to smaller community hospitals/nursing homes to enable the closure of the asylums?' The answer was still being sought in 1983, when the Department of Health and Social Security (DHSS) launched a programme of pilot *Care in the Community* projects to follow its earlier guidance. A central allocation of £19 million was made available to fund twenty-eight locally based resettlement projects distributed around

England. These were to provide a variety of community placements for up to 900 people languishing as long-stay inpatients. The community facilities would range from ordinary houses to group homes and hostels.[44]

At the same time some attempt was made to try to isolate those large hospitals which were really too deteriorated and poorly situated to continue. Government attempts to define such hospitals did of course give a new lease of life to those not under scrutiny. Health authorities were thus urged to

> Make arrangements satisfactory to patients and staff locally for the closure over the next ten years or so of those mental illness hospitals which are not well placed to provide a service reaching out into the community and are already near the end of their useful life. Such closures should provide a source of staff, capital and revenue to support the development of the new pattern of health services, including community psychiatric nursing, for the mentally ill *and perhaps help to support the development of services provided by local authorities*.[45] (my emphasis)

By 1988 firm closure programmes had been devised for 43 out of 178 hospital units for mentally ill patients in England surveyed by the National Schizophrenia Fellowship (NSF).[46] However, at the time of writing there is some doubt about the robustness of these programmes while the implications of the internal marketing reform in the NHS are worked through.

Social policy and community care

In 1986 the government appointed Sir Roy Griffiths, the private sector consultant behind the earlier general management reforms in the NHS, to carry out an inquiry into community care.[47] The primary concerns were twofold. First, spending on residential care in private sector homes for elderly people through the social security budget was rising at an exponential rate and was to all intents and purposes out of control, being demand led. Reports on residential care indicated that its quality was extremely variable and that monitoring arrangements were far from satisfactory. Second, the development of community care facilities was extremely patchy and there was a widespread belief that the policy, aside from the isolated initiatives such as the DHSS pilot projects, was simply not working

As the government itself was to admit in its response to the resultant Griffiths Report on Community Care, the 'rapid growth of residential and nursing home care' had been 'unplanned and largely based on the availability of social security benefits'.[48] This indicated that transinstitutionalization might be taking place. There were also fears that the same trends of homelessness among mentally ill people as had become apparent in the USA were being repeated in Britain.

The reforms proposed by Griffiths to remedy the situation are discussed further in the conclusion. The important factor for the mental hospitals was that the Minister for Health gave what he called the 'amber light' to authorities planning reprovision of services in the community. The secretary of state meanwhile pledged himself to ensure that discharges of seriously mentally ill people from hospital would take place only when adequate medical and social care was available for them outside hospital.[49]

The Griffiths inquiry stemmed also from broader concerns in the provision of welfare in the late twentieth century. The ideal of privatized, familial, informal care, unsullied by the peremptory intervention of the municipality, has been pursued with some vigour.

Knapp draws out five significant themes in the development of care in the community initiatives. These are de-hospitalization, joint working (between the NHS local authorities), cost-effectiveness, consumerism and 'mixing the economy'.[50] He suggests that the search for cost-effectiveness was particularly prevalent in the 1980s, with the establishment of the Audit Commission and the development of performance indicators in the NHS. Though a laudable objective, it came to be identified with health and local authorities seeking to make savings by passing costs of care to the social security budget maintained by central government.

Consumerism embraces new forms of individualized care planning such as case management through which the recipient of the service will be involved in decision-making. The aim is to allow consumers to have greater influence over forms of care allotted to them. The Disabled Persons Act 1986 enshrined the new principles, though without providing funds for the advocacy arrangements desired.

The mixing of the economy, the last of Knapp's five themes, is probably the most important in terms of future social policy. A key response of governments in Europe to the perceived fiscal crisis of the mid-1970s was to adopt strategies which would restrain state expenditure, switch payment for utilities from taxation to consumer charging, and allow the private and voluntary sectors to play a larger role in the provision of transport, education and welfare services.

An interesting early example of the attempt to empower consumers and strengthen the role of the private sector was the 1975 initiative of Kent County Council to test the viability of a voucher scheme for school places. The move came about under the stimulus of 'national debate on educational standards, finance and accountability'.[51]

The scheme was not adopted and the results of the feasibility study provide a good example of some of the difficulties that the state has faced in attempting to change the pattern of welfare. First, it was estimated that the annual cost of the scheme to the Council would possibly be of the order of £1.25 million. The only possible savings would be from reductions in the number of teachers in the maintained schools, which would come about if parents were to stick to the survey preferences that they indicated for the independent sector. These savings were thought to be of the order of £0.5 million at the most.

Second, parents did not choose to vary their choice of schools for their children in the hypothetical voucher system in any marked way from their choices of placements under the then existing system. Only 12 per cent of parents interviewed chose a different school from the one currently attended; the majority opted to remain in the maintained sector.

The reason for highlighting this instance of attempted change can now be made clear. Writers such as Hill and Bramley and Duncan and Goodwin have contested the idea that an economic *crisis* occurred in the 1970s.[52] Significant public spending restraint had in fact been introduced earlier in the 1960s under the Wilson government. The search for alternative means of supplying services might derive its urgency from perceived rather than real crisis, and more particularly a disenchantment with state social planning as such. This fed the general enthusiasm for liberating people from the too close supervision of the state, and in turn ushered in the rise of Hayek's system of philosophy in which the aim is to reduce government provision to the barest minimum, for civil security and basic social security only. All other systems of social support should be for voluntary organizations of citizens to devise and subscribe to.[53]

The OECD (Organization for Economic Co-operation and Development) has recently argued that governments are not likely to be successful in securing increased public sector efficiency unless there is a greater role for the price mechanism and market forces. This is on the grounds that people who value services 'will consume as much as they are willing to pay for'.[54] Charging for services, especially public transport, refuse collection and street cleaning, is therefore considered to offer considerable scope for increasing efficiency. Particularly noted is the case of the former Federal Republic of Germany (FRG), where local governments raise a quarter of their income from charging, mostly through environment and public health levies. Nevertheless the OECD cautions that principles of equity do impose a limit to the possibilities for charging.

Probably the most striking shift from the public to the private sector not only in Britain, but also in France and the USA has taken place in the provision of housing. The growth of home ownership has enjoyed cross-party support in Parliament. The desire to own a home was considered 'deep and natural' by the Conservatives, and 'basic and natural' by the Labour party.[55] Housing was the first of the public sector programmes to be tied back in the 1960s. This has had important consequences for the rehabilitation of mental hospital patients, which will be discussed in the context of the empirical study reported in Chapters 3, 4 and 5.

The search for alternatives to the failed British system of state provision led Segalman and Marsland to look for, and find, a welfare idyll in Switzerland.[56] The Swiss do not have a national health service and most of the population is covered by voluntary health insurance. Segalman and

Marsland were struck by the fact that the Swiss appear to have 'no concept of a right to state support'. Rigorous means testing is 'carried out without difficulty' and public aid can be recovered if a person later becomes affluent. The observers were also especially impressed by the collective concern for those who showed signs of being unable to support themselves at the local level:

> If a child should begin to falter in [occupational training] for adult self-sufficiency, the whole community becomes concerned – not just the school's personnel, but the whole gamut of formal and informal social control mechanisms become actively involved.[57]

The remedies which they prescribe for Britain involve the separation of social insurance for health, pensions and employment from social assistance to those in unpredictable need. Financial responsibility for giving support would be delegated to a local level in order to rekindle civic responsibility.

But looking back to the principles of Beveridge's plan for welfare, one of the main conditions which the originators made, in order that a workable system might evolve, was that reasonably full employment be maintained. Neither high levels of endemic unemployment, nor its corollary, mass dependence on benefits was envisaged.[58] Segalman and Marsland take little account of this issue.

Achieving regular employment has been one of the most difficult targets for people who have left institutions and there is a marked descent through the occupational and class structure so that, especially where they have suffered illnesses such as schizophrenia, the work they are able to get tends to be of an unskilled or semi-skilled kind. At the same time, the opportunities available are often for casual work rather than permanent positions. This raises issues about the conditions of employment within such work and to what extent they are associated with exploitation and vulnerability.

Within the European context Britain has always had a relatively large 'marginal workforce'. Part-time workers accounted for only 7 per cent of the employed population in France and between 10 and 12 per cent in the former FRG during the 1960s and early 1970s. For the same period in Britain these workers made up 20 per cent of the workforce. At the same time there was a 'well-established tradition to use temporary labour'.[59] Lane argues that up to the middle of the 1970s the conditions of employment of part-time and temporary workers were reasonably protected by the state balancing the interests of capital and labour. But at that point, 'the general deterioration of economic development, the growing uncertainty and instability on world product markets and the introduction of new technology brought about new requirements in the utilisation of labour, as well as mass unemployment'. An important part of the new model was what Lane calls the 'restoration of worker competition for employment'.[60]

In France the new model – which Lane calls 'market capitalism' to distinguish it from the welfare capitalism of the previous period – led to a number of legislative changes. These lifted some of the restrictions attaching to contracts, such as those involving precarious employment outside the state sector or fixed-term and other like kinds of less secure employment. In Britain there was a significant reduction in the number of employees eligible for employment protection, so that to be within the terms of the Employment Protection Act, they had to be working for two years instead of, as previously, six months. The already high percentage of part-time workers increased to 23 per cent and 'there occurred a small to moderate increase in the proportion of temporary workers'.[61]

Thus on balance marginal and less protected forms of employment have not grown at any marked rate in the market capitalism phase that Lane distinguishes. What is important is the change in conditions of those employments which clearly are of one kind in making the marginal workforce more vulnerable. As Lane points out, surveys suggest that a majority of temporary workers actually opt for temporary status by choice, but nevertheless a large proportion are in fact disadvantaged since they lack the benefits which attach to permanent positions.

This employment context of increased competition between applicants for insecure part-time or fixed-term jobs with few protective conditions, suggests that the ideals of rehabilitation and normalization – that is the restoration of opportunities for participation in all areas of civil society – will be extremely difficult to implement within the terms of hospital rundown. This brings us back to the underlying issue in this chapter about welfare and dependency. Normalization requires equality of outcome as a fundamental principle, and indeed therapeutic right. For clients of the services for mentally ill people, protection of conditions of employment to work toward that outcome is important. The withdrawal of state protection for the marginal workforce makes adherence to that principle problematic.

Summary

The search for alternatives to state welfare provision, and in particular for informal, privatized, familial and voluntary care to be substituted, forms a foundation for the move away from mental hospitals. As this review of change in Europe and the USA has shown, there were a number of important experiments in the 1940s and 1950s which, coincident with the development of mood-stabilizing drugs, suggested that a significant number of long-term patients could be successfully boarded out in the community. Yet local authorities seemed to exhibit a universal lack of interest in developing alternative services to the mental hospitals, even when given sizeable subsidies. At the same time the insurers who supported much mental hospital care under the continental system were not willing to finance non-medical social support. Where action did occur, in the USA and Italy, in each case a central government initiative drove the process of local reform. In the USA it was the federal programme for mental health centres fuelled by a faith in the capacity of psychiatrists to improve the health of the nation. In Italy the campaign of the Radical party achieved legislation to stop admissions to the mental hospitals.

The availability of subsidies for care, whether through insurance companies or state schemes has acted both as an obstacle to change and as a change facilitator. In France, the former FRG and The Netherlands, the guaranteed subsidy for medical treatment gave the hospitals a secure role provided they could attract sufficient customers. In the USA and to a limited extent in Britain, the availability of subsidies for nursing home care has encouraged a transfer of patients away from the long-stay institutions, and thus the more advanced pace of rundown in those two countries.

The perceived fiscal crisis of the mid-1970s and 'stagflation' in the USA brought in their train attempts to limit state expenditure on welfare. The difference in attitudes toward welfare between the USA and Europe has been highlighted to show that trends toward contraction of municipal housing and urban programmes, when coupled with the process of deinstitutionalization, make it more likely that hospital leavers will be marginalized in a competitive environment. The themes Knapp picks out about community care, the mixing of the economy and the drive to cut municipal costs, viewed in the light of the OECD concern to develop customer charging for services, assume a market among those with long-term illnesses or needs for support. This has been contested by many students of welfare systems. The experience in housing and nursing home care in Britain suggests that the level of state subsidies required to enable poor individuals to participate in such a market does not lead to a reduction in the total cost to the state. The picture is obscured by the different public and private agencies seeking to divest themselves of the burden by distributing costs between one another.

De-hospitalization can be seen as a natural consequence of the decline in numbers of old long-stay patients. To this extent closures can be seen to stem from therapeutic advances achieved by professional care staff. But then it is puzzling why so little reduction has occurred in Europe as a whole. The professions in psychiatry are not convinced of the therapeutic advantages of the move to the community, hence the suggestion from within that fraternity that rehabilitation is something of a myth. Clearly more weight attaches to the principal administrative and economic factors: the development of general hospital treatment and primary care which are intended to replace mental hospitals, and the search for more cost-effective alternatives to state hospital provision. Since the new forms of treatment set up have not reduced the demand for state hospital admissions and the alternatives so far devised have not guaranteed more cost-effective services, the move into the community can be seen to be reaching a critical stage of development.

Italy and the USA constitute rogue cases in the sense that in the former case there was political interest in change, while in the latter case there was an extraordinary mass interest in psychiatry. In Britain the process was subject to much more diffidence and restraint. But this is to anticipate the next chapter.

References

1 Bassuk, E.L. (1978). Deinstitutionalization and mental health services, *Scientific American* 238, 2: 46–53.
2 Bachrach, L.L. (1978). A conceptual approach to deinstitutionalization, *Hospital and Community Psychiatry* 29, 9: 574.
3 ibid.: 575–6.
4 Kirk, S.A. and Therrien, M.E. (1975). Community mental health myths and the fate of former hospitalized patients, *Psychiatry* 38: 209–17.
5 Lamb, H.R. and Grant, R.W. (1982). The mentally ill in an urban county jail, *Archives of General Psychiatry* 39: 17–22.
  Lamb, H.R. (1989). Deinstitutionalization at the Crossroads, *Hospital and Community Psychiatry* 39: 941–5.
  Brown, P. (1985). *The Transfer of Care*, London, Routledge & Kegan Paul.
6 Buss, T.F. and Redburn, F.S. (1983). *Plant Closings and Community Mental Health*, Beverly Hills, Calif., Sage, p. 196.
7 Bassuk (1978), p. 49.
8 Musto, D.F. (1977). The community mental health movement in historical perspective, in W.E. Barton and C.J. Sanborn (eds) *An Assessment of the Community Mental Health Movement*, Lexington, Mass., D.C.
  Heath, cited in Buss and Redburn (1983), p. 199.
9 Gardner, E.A. (1977). Community mental health centre movement: learning from failure, in Barton and Sanborn (1977), cited in Buss and Redburn (1983), p. 202.
10 Jones, K. and Poletti, A. (1985). Understanding the Italian experience, *British Journal of Psychiatry* 146: 341–7.
  —— (1986). The Italian experience reconsidered, *British Journal of Psychiatry* 148: 144–50.
11 Bollini, P. and Mollica, R.F. (1989). Surviving without the asylum, *Journal of Nervous and Mental Disease* 177, 10: 607.
12 Ramon, S. (1983). Psychiatria democratia: a case study of the Italian community mental health service, *International Journal of Health Services* 13, 2: 311.
13 Perris, C. and Kemali, D. (eds) (1985). Focus on the Italian psychiatric reform, *Acta Psychiatrica Scandinavica* Supplementum 316: 71.
14 Dell'Acqua, G. and Cogliati Dezza, M.G. (1985). The end of the mental hospital: a review of the psychiatric experience in Trieste, in Perris and Kemali (1985), p. 51.
15 ibid., pp. 51–2.
16 Ramon (1983), p. 320.

17 Shapiro, R.Y. and Young, J.T. (1989). Public opinion and the welfare state: the U.S. in comparative perspective, *Political Science Quarterly* 104, 1: 59–89.

18 ibid.: 73.

19 Dear, M. and Wolch, J. (1989). *Landscapes of Despair: From Deinstitutionalization to Homelessness*, London, Polity Press.

20 Marmor, T.R. (1986). The political and economic context of mental health care in the US, Paper presented to a Conference held at the Center for Advanced Study in the Behavioral Sciences, Stanford, California, on 'Innovations in Mental Health Care Delivery in the U.S.A. and the U.K. Impediments and Implementation', 13–15 November, p. 22.

21 ibid., p. 33.

22 Atherton, C.R. (1989). The Welfare State: still on solid ground, *Social Service Review* June: 167–79.

23 Andalusian Institution for Mental Health (1989). *Psychiatric Reform in Andalusia*, Spain, Junta de Andalucia.

24 Sarantidis, D. and Tripodinakis, J. (1989). Starting point in the reform of psychiatric care in Greece, Paper presented to a Regional Symposium of the World Psychiatric Association held in Granada, Spain, on 'Mental Health Community Services', 29 March to 1 April.

25 Ribeiro, N.A. (1987). Planning proposal of the mental health and psychiatric delivery care sub system of the metropolitan areas, Paper presented to a Symposium held at the Hotel Tivoli, Lisbon on 'Portuguese-Swedish Cooperation in Hospital Planning and Technology', 6 November.

26 Giel, R. (1986). Care of chronic mental patients in The Netherlands, *Social Psychiatry* 21: 25.

27 Verbraak, P. (1990). Mental health care in The Netherlands, Presentation to a meeting at Friern Hospital, London, 4 May.

28 Van der Grinten, T. (1985). Mental health care in The Netherlands, in S.P. Mangen (ed.) *Mental Health Care in the European Community*, London, Croom Helm, pp. 211–12.

29 Gersons, B.P.R. (1987). Psychiatric emergency services within programmes for community rehabilitation, Paper presented to a Conference of the World Health Organization at Amsterdam, The Netherlands, on 'Research and Innovative Practices for Community Rehabilitation of Persons with Chronic Mental Illness', 29–31 October, p. 5.

30 Giel (1986): 25, 32.

31 Mangen, S.P. and Castel, K. (1985). France: the psychiatrie de secteur, in Mangen (1985), p. 118.

32 ibid., p. 120.

33 ibid., p. 144.

34 ibid., p. 149.

35 Martin, F.M. (1984). *Between the Acts: Community Mental Health Services 1959–1983*, London, Nuffield Provincial Hospitals Trust.

36 Beresford, P. and Croft, S. (1986). *Whose Welfare?*, Brighton Polytechnic, Lewis Cohen Urban Studies Unit.

37 Thomas, D.N. (1983). *The Making of Community Work*, London, Allen & Unwin.

38 Hunter, D.J. (1980). *Coping with Uncertainty*, Letchworth, John Riley.

39 DHSS (1976). *Priorities for Health and Personal Social Services in England: a Consultative Document*, London, HMSO.
40 DHSS (1981). *Care in the Community: A Consultative Document on Moving Resources for Care in England*, London, HMSO, para 3.2.
41 DHSS (1975). *Better Services for the Mentally Ill*, London, HMSO, para 11.10.
42 DHSS/Welsh Office (1969). *The Functions of the District General Hospital*, London, HMSO.
43 DHSS (1977). *Priorities in Health and Personal Social Services: The Way Forward*, London, HMSO, p. 9.
44 Knapp, M., Cambridge, P., Thomason C., *et al.* (1990). *Care in the Community: Lessons from a Demonstration Programme*, Canterbury, University of Kent Personal Social Services Research Unit.
45 DHSS (1981). *Care in Action: A Handbook of Policies and Priorities for the Health and Personal Social Services in England*, London, HMSO, para 5.9.
46 Mauthner, N. (1988). *Report on Hospital Closures*, Surbiton, National Schizophrenia Fellowship.
47 Griffiths, R. (1988). *Community Care: Agenda for Action*, London, HMSO.
48 Department of Health (1989). *Health Services Management: Government response to the Griffiths Report on Community Care*, London, HMSO, para 5.
49 DSS (1989). *Statement: Mental Illness Initiative*, 13 July.
50 Knapp, M. (1988). Construction and expectation: themes from the Care in the Community Initiative, in P. Cambridge and M. Knapp (eds) *Demonstrating Successful Care in the Community*, Canterbury, University of Kent Personal Social Services Research Unit.
51 Kent County Council (1978). *Education Vouchers in Kent: A Feasibility Study for the Education Department of the Kent County Council*, Maidstone, Kent County Council.
52 Hill, M. and Bramley, G. (1986). *Analysing Social Policy*, Oxford, Basil Blackwell.
   Duncan, S. and Goodwin, M. *The Local State and Uneven Development*, Oxford, Polity Press in association with Basil Blackwell.
53 Hayek, F.A. (1944). *The Road to Serfdom*, London, Routledge & Kegan Paul.
54 OECD (1987). *Managing and Financing Urban Services*, Paris, OECD.
55 Willmott, P. and Murie, A. (1988). *Polarisation and Social Housing*, London, Policy Studies Institute, p. 20.
56 Segalman, R. and Marsland, D. (1989). *Cradle to Grave: Comparative Perspectives on the State of Welfare*, Basingstoke, Macmillan in association with the Social Affairs Unit.
57 ibid., p. 67.
58 Beveridge, W.H. (1942). *Social Insurance and Allied Service*, London, HMSO.
59 Lane, C. (1989). From welfare capitalism to market capitalism: a comparative review of trends towards employment flexibility in the labour markets of three major European societies, *Sociology* 23, 4: 583–610.
60 ibid.: 590.
61 ibid.: 595.

2

A theoretical framework

The overview of mental health policy in the USA and Europe presented in Chapter 1 suggests that in many aspects the British case is typical of the continental process of reform. No political movement has emerged in Britain to press for rundown of the mental hospitals. Psychiatrists have not been involved in the lobbying of Parliament to any significant degree. As Cooper wryly observes:

> It is often not appreciated, at least in the U.K. that the medical profession has had very little say in the major decisions about the design of the health services. For instance nobody knows who provided the detailed advice upon which 'Better Services for the Mentally Ill' [the blueprint for government policy published in 1975] was based.

He continues

> Similarly, mental hospitals were not built at the suggestion of psychiatrists, and psychiatrists have not been responsible as a profession for their run-down and closure.[1]

While the Royal College of Psychiatrists and the British Medical Association counselled caution on closures, the impressive period architecture of asylums has attracted the interest of architects in the possibilities of preserving them intact with a resident population.[2]

No national directive on the hospitals has been issued to the effect that there should be no further patient admissions to any of them. As the case of Italy indicates, even if there had been, researchers would have had to examine the activity of the local state very closely to establish what action had been taken upon the directive.

This raises the issue of centre–locality conflict. For some time in social policy it has been appreciated that local administrations do not simply act as transmitters of national legislation and guidance. Aside from issues of

National concern to preserve the Victorian architectural heritage has drawn attention to the possibilities of asylum recycling

interpretation and priorities between the directives, Barrett and Fudge have described local implementation as falling within a policy–action continuum.[3] The existence of the continuum means that policies made by the centre are changed by information and guidance coming back up from the locality.

Drawing on an analysis of American inter-organizational relations Lindblom argues that it is simply not possible for the central state to impose its wishes on the local state.[4] Marmor's discussion of the incipient federalism of the USA's fifty states, and popular distrust of national government, lends support to such a view.[5] Lindblom's main point is that where local policy-makers have not made the decisions they will be slow to take action to implement them, and the significant degree of local state autonomy on questions of social policy suggests that this would be a situation easy to envisage. This process of policy-shaping is held to be legitimate because the local state has to react to popular pressures in devising its welfare systems. The dominant American view is that interest groups will always be able to organize themselves where the need arises and to defend their social position before the state. This is seen as a natural process of democracy.

The potential anarchy and irresponsible policy deviation of this situation – where the local bullies and barons of federal funding set the agenda – is not so apparent as might seem however. Government's most cherished social policies may be enforced against local opposition, whether through the courts, dismissal of authorities which fail to set budgets, or through the imposition of 'direct rule' over a recalcitrant agency. In Britain rate and poll-tax capping are obvious examples of such action by the centre. Palmer views these types of key policies for central government, which it is willing to enforce strongly, as 'strategic highs'.[6] Where the implementation of such strategic highs is in question the centre will limit the action space around interpretability and local discretion. Within the NHS the Government requirement for ancillary services to be offered to private as well as 'in house' tenders can be considered one such strategic objective. Ham's research indicates that government ministers played a more important role than local administrators in determining the course of implementation of this initiative.[7]

The American theory of autonomic development of interest group pressures to ensure equitable state policy outcomes draws attention to the shape of popular pressures of health services. Alford's work indicates that in the USA three principal interest groups are involved.[8] 'Professional monopolists' attempt to retain a system in which the location, costs and type of service is determined by those who provide it, primarily doctors, 'Corporate rationalizers', the second interest group, are the planners and administrators of health organizations who attempt to achieve a rational spread of services to meet the socio-demographic distribution of need. Alford distinguishes the lay popular interest in development of services as the third and largely repressed force: it is not organized as a permanent lobby and is not party to the agenda setting between the monopolists and the rationalizers.

The system of interest group pressure ensuring state responsiveness to its publics thus appears to be flawed. Bachrach and Baratz posit the existence of 'institutional dominance' in large corporations.[9] This dominance exhibits itself in the ability of corporations to choose effectively which topics of policy they will shepherd into the arena of public debate, and which they will keep within the confines of private discussions. Public consultation about policies can therefore be something of a sham where major options and potential developments are either not shared with the public by the corporation or not conceptualized by the public.

Nevertheless the structure of the planning process within the district health authorities (DHAs) of the NHS has given wide scope for public interests to be admitted. Institutional dominance is not a necessary condition of policy-making. The process established in 1982 provides that 'bodies with a close interest should be consulted informally throughout the development of plans and programmes' and that 'the body in question may be represented on the planning team'. With regard to formal consultation it is stipulated that 'professional advisory committees, academic authorities, bodies representing the interests of staff, CHCs [community health councils] and local authorities will be included, *as well as any other relevant interests*' (my emphasis).[10]

The Barclay and Cumberledge reports on social work and nursing respectively laid strong emphasis on patch-based working for the 1980s.[11] The parish or ward base – the patch, neighbourhood or most recently 'locality' – has become the fashionable location for the receiving and giving of care. While this is often assumed axiomatic to good services, which have been removed from a local base only because of the division of labour requirements of bureaux, it is not a self-evident welfare virtue. It can remove choice and increase stigma. It can make the relation between the carer and the person cared for too familiar. For mentally ill people local care may be undesirable if they wish to be treated by anonymous carers rather than people who may live in their own locality. Relatives who are carers may also find that the requirement for professional support to be given locally infringes on their own rights to privacy. They may fear that the condition of the person they care for might become common knowledge in the neighbourhood, and prefer the anonymity afforded by distant, specialized, non-local treatment facilities. In fact these difficulties are not restricted to the giving and receiving of care, but are also reflected more generally in phenomena of social contact and recognition between neighbours.

In the 1970s Abrams and colleagues carried out the 'Street studies' of neighbouring and subsequently reviewed neighbourhood care schemes.[12] Abrams believed neighbouring to hang on a dilemma which those who live near to each other have between the need for support in times of crisis and the need for privacy. While neighbours need to contribute to some notional 'stock of common good', so that they can draw on it should they become in need of help at some point in the future, they also wish not to be imposed upon by the needs of others.[13]

As Marsden commented in the discussion of Abrams's original research proposals:

> At the most general conceptual level of what we mean by good neigh-bouring, the ideas are tapping very thorny problems of the sources of social cohesion and solidarity. For instance if you translate 'neigh-bourly behaviour' into 'altruism' or 'community' you are immediate-ly into all the problems discussed from Tönnies and Durkheim onwards (i.e. how and why solidarity is built upon kinship, common place, occupation, religion and so on). And if you look at studies of 'community' it seems to me that they haven't been resolved.[14]

Corporatism and post-Fordism have led to the control of industry, employ-ment and markets from international centres which supervise the socio-economic development of continental trading communities. There is little scope for such matters to be controlled from within neighbourhoods by the people living within them. With the increasing emphasis on provision of housing and transport outside the state, these goods too are increasingly distributed and rationed along such lines. In the light of these trends the concepts of neighbourhood or patch have become less relevant to civic self-determination. Locality on the other hand has come into the ascendancy because of the need to redefine forces for local autonomy around much larger clusters of population. The localities described by Cooke and col-leagues are essentially local market-places competing with others in the international network. He defines locality as

> the space within which the larger part of most citizens' daily working and consuming lives is lived. It is the base for a large measure of individual and social mobilization to activate, extend or defend those rights, not simply in the political sphere but more generally in the areas of cultural, economic and social life.[15]

This theme of giving back control over civic affairs to local people and moving away from the grip of town halls and utility or service administra-tions was one investigated in the community development projects of the 1970s. Analysis of these projects suggested that if such control were to be achieved, local people would have to acquire the motivation and skills to be able to organize themselves into effective action groups able to negoti-ate with public authorities. These skills are not common and are mostly cultivated by middle-class residents who do not live in the areas most in need of a collective uplift. There seems little hope of local control of health issues in the inner city.

The unlikelihood of the urban parish continuing to exhibit the features of a self-standing community has also been revealed by research showing the way in which kinship and friendship contacts are kept up over ever increasing geographical distances, largely because of mass car and telephone ownership.[16]

Community care co-ordinated from Brussels and delivered into neighbourhoods by the corporate providers of the European Community would seem the final blow to the familial, private and intimately local ideal. Higgins among others has called for the abandonment of the term 'community care' and for the identification of practical alternatives.[17] However, health authorities and family practitioner authorities are keen on the idea of generic teams delivering patch-based care. Localism is seen as a good thing in itself. With their populations of 100,000 to 300,000, health districts offer the possibility of considerable demographic subdivision, according to ethnic mix, the proportion of elderly people living alone, the proportion of young people in the population and so on. But this idea of care in the locality is little different from one which follows the need for an effective division of labour to be adopted by health maintenance organizations. What is confusing about locality is the romance attached to the concept which implies that remote governments have somehow been thrust off by street corner society.

Drawing together the threads of this discussion of community, neighbourhood and locality care, it is possible to construct a simple theoretical framework for study of the empirical question at hand, the closure of two large English mental hospitals. The framework can be best seen in terms of a continuum of discretion. At one end of the continuum, local actors within centre-controlled authorities have no discretion. The policies for health and social services are dictated from central government, and health authorities and local government simply implement them. The scope of their action is fixed by universally applicable criteria. At the other end of the continuum, local actors have a large area of discretion within what can be termed 'Athenian' authorities. In implementing and interpreting policies, they challenge the imposition of legal obligations where they feel it is locally valid to do so. Representatives of Athenian local states purposively seek to nurture popular campaigns and public initiatives which can take up the welfare services 'action space'. The role of the authority itself is then one of free-ranging facilitating and monitoring.

Between these opposite ends of the continuum lie intermediary kinds of local state action which I have termed guided, autarchic and decentralized (see Figure 1). Constructed as ideal types, they are in Weber's famous phrase 'one-sided accentuations of reality'. In the 'real process' of policy implementation, local authorities may follow a pattern of action drawing on several of the types sketched here. But by distinguishing clearly between them in this methodological fashion it is possible to explore how far local state action tends to fall into one type rather than another when action on any one policy is considered.

Figure 1 A continuum of discretion

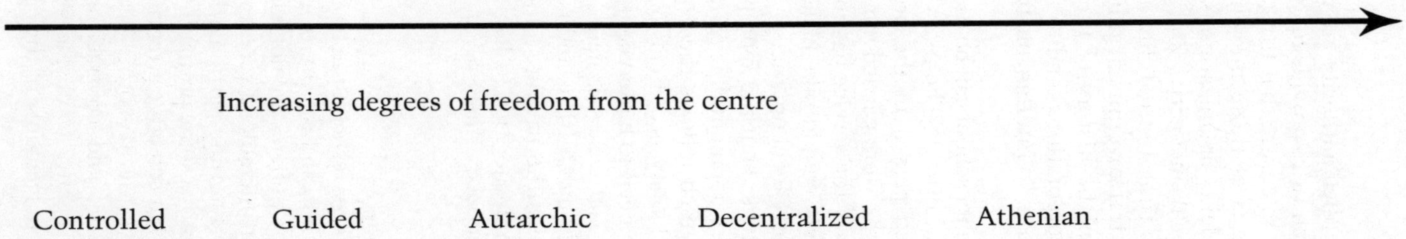

Increasing degrees of freedom from the centre

Controlled   Guided   Autarchic   Decentralized   Athenian

The controlled authority

The characteristics of the controlled authority are in some ways those of the classic bureaucracy, in which rules provide for all cases of need. They are impartially applied in order to ensure that the goals of welfare are not subverted to the partial concerns of those implementing policy. While appropriate for armies, this model of organization is widely believed to be too inflexible, remote, impersonal, ineffective and inefficient for welfare provision. However, unelected, time limited, hierarchical agencies have played an important role in central government initiatives to solve social problems. This is illustrated in the history of the Urban Development Corporations in Britain. Such corporations tend to usurp the functions of local elected authorities which are simultaneously subjected to greater central control.

The action research of the Brunel school can be used to draw out the key advantages of the controlled authority.[18] The main theme is that the duties and responsibilities of each person in the organization are unambiguously defined. To this end the work carried out is divided into levels. At the grass-roots, the deliverer of the service has to make no judgements about when or where the delivery should take place. This is already prescribed for him or her. At the next level up, that of 'situational response', professionals need to take decisions about the appropriateness of particular forms of follow-up. The third 'developmental' level involves choices about the organization of workload which follows these professional decisions about action. At the fourth level analysis of fields of need is carried out at the top of the organization. The need to be served is in turn prescribed, in this instance, by the centre. In one sense this definition of fields of needs was attempted rather graphically by Griffiths and is a feature of the NHS and Community Care Bill. Local authorities are to take charge of responding to social care needs, health authorities to health care needs, with a fairly firmly defined boundary between the two.

The guided authority

The concept of the guided authority rests on the traditions of independent local government, voluntary action, and the use of expert opinion in decision making about welfare. Many policies are not based on rule books and central government allows considerable discretion to the local state. Though the 1988–1991 welfare reforms, particularly those in Education and the NHS, have tended to remove some of that discretion, nevertheless central government pays somewhat selective attention to the issues which it sees as the most politically pressing. The others are left to the localities. In many respects the purchasing and contracting arrangements have strengthened the power of the locality to decide, mainly because of the reliance placed on the technical judgements of the caring professions.

Implementation in the guided authority is thus a messier affair than in the controlled authority. The political aims of the centre are not written on tablets of stone and handed down from the Mount. Some areas of policy may be the subject only of unspecific recommendations, perhaps setting out a range of loosely worded options. In turn these open up the field to considerable latitude of local interpretation. The guidance may in any case often be dated. Within its terms local actors are able to develop independent initiatives, such as, for example, those involving health care for women.

The theory of guided authorities draws its strength from Glennerster's work on social planning for elderly and mentally handicapped people.[19] The Centre for Corporate Strategy and Change also tends to implicitly adopt this model.[20] It recognizes that professional decision-makers often form themselves into factions for the purposes of bargaining. They also seek to become owners of policy initiatives rather than to act as transmitters for central political goals. The pursuit of localism as a phenomenon within state organizational cultures reinforces these tendencies. The competition between professional and management groups is seen as essentially productive, and indeed is the stuff of life for those inhabiting the organizational levels. It is particularly important for innovations and community care. As Stocking has shown, an innovation may be shown to be effective but not adopted widely, whereas another innovation may not have been demonstrated to be effective yet can become widely accepted in practice.[21] The differences seem to be to do with the fact that local 'product champions' are often required to stimulate the infusion of new practices. These champions need to enjoy both a senior position and the respect of colleagues outside their own profession.

Glennerster suggests that the centre should give incentives to the localities to encourage the healthy competiveness for innovations. For example the centre could facilitate research in the areas where it felt that development, change and adoption of new techniques was required. Discretionary policy-making at a number of levels in the organization is thus the key to this system, perhaps corresponding in its *internal* fluidity to some of the features of Burns and Stalker's organic model of organization.[22]

The autarchic authority

The autarchic authority is one which brings to mind Marmor's image of the agrarian, government distrusting USA. Local states are not accorded a leading role in decisions about welfare. Expertise is diffuse rather than held within the guided hand of the state authority. As a mixed economy of welfare emerges in Britain, clearly the model of the autarchic authority will assume greater significance. While the negotiation of outcomes between central government and local government is important, proposals are not generated directly from factions or product champions *internal* to the authorities concerned. Rather they are formed within an *external* market of inter-agency competition and adjustment. In order to determine its policy, each local state authority is constantly adjusting its position to take account of the intentions of others. At the same time it also has to adjust to market leaders in the private and voluntary sectors and to public interest groups. Here prescription from the centre is most unwelcome.

On one level the policy of local agencies evolves in a way that is 'disjointed' and 'incremental' and could be seen as the antithesis of responsible party policy-making.[23] On another level policies are not irrational and their disjointed character is not seen as a bad thing by the apologists of incrementalism. They regard the conflicts between the centre and the locality as inevitable. Compromises would not attract the support of the key interest groups in either and would be impossible to implement. Ideally the conflicts are thus best resolved by non-negotiated partisan action taken by one agency in anticipation of, or in response to, the actions of another. Management of welfare thus follows the course of a large chess game. Where two agencies put forward conflicting options, the search is inevitably on for a third option, which may involve negotiation. These processes are justified by the fact that the audience wields some power over the moves of the managers. Organized interest groups play a significant part in the decisions.

Critics point to the disservice to the public of allowing the self-interest of organizations to determine welfare outcomes. Benson for instance argues that agencies are primarily concerned with achieving what he calls an 'uncluttered domain' for their services.[24] The problems posed by the resultant institutional dominance are not addressed. The public support which any of the agencies enjoys for its services will depend on the social rank and size of social groups which can be mobilized to defend it. The strength of agencies will thus not necessarily reflect the popularity of their policies. Autarchic manoeuvrings at the inter-organizational level thus leave open the issue of 'localism'. This is for a more radical type of authority to pursue.

The decentralized authority

A strategy of decentralization would appear to answer the critics of monolithic bureaux and self-serving power and resources maximizers. Authorities following this strategy are less vulnerable to the control of professional groups or corporate interests and correspondingly more open to popular pressure. The means of power and decision-making in the decentralized authority are made freely available to non-state agencies and other organized interest groups. Opportunities for influence and participation are thus not dependent on the social rank or size of such groups. A number of authorities in Britain have attempted to devise means of sharing decision-making with neighbourhood groups, Islington and Walsall Councils being among the first to do so.

In the interpretation of national guidance and development of local responses, the members of a decentralizing authority

> take seriously the possibility of institutional dominance posed by the existence of their own and other welfare organisations ... they would be concerned to consider options for change which challenge the vested interest, or the market position of their organisation itself – for instance by acting as subordinate partner to other agencies in a cooperative venture.[25]

The decentralized authority has a somewhat dated ring to it, in that it retains a faith in the ability of the local state to decide and provide. However, decentralization raises an important theme for the empirical processes to be outlined in the next three chapters. This centres on Bachrach and Baratz's suggestion that public bodies resort to appeals to 'symbolic normative values' to foist off challenges to their own values.[26] A lot of work is put into making organizational procedures resistant to public manipulation of the decision-making. For decentralization to work, state policies should reflect the desires of outside interest groups at the sub authority level. The local state has to resist its tendencies to manipulate. As in the case of autarchic policy making, effective outside influence would require that public interest in specific social issues had already been articulated (rather than being reflected in some generalized public unease). In the decentralizing authority the exercise of that influence is made much easier by the offer of *participant* status in the administration and development of local policy.

The Athenian authority

At one remove from decentralization is the Athenian model of action which lies at the least controlled end of the continuum. For Athenian authorities, sharing of power and admission of non-state interests is not sufficient because it allows influence only to the articulate and to civic agitators – the minority who can turn municipal decision-making to their own advantage. Social groups which lack the civic skills to represent their own interests are particularly vulnerable to neglect by decentralizing agencies. This is an important point where chronic mentally ill people are concerned, since many lack the confidence and social skills to make a telling case for their needs to be met. So, an athenian democracy where all have a voice is required. This may take two principal forms. In the first, the state facilitates the democratic organization of clients. Ideally the pressure groups formed are not to be organized functionally around 'clienthood' or 'patienthood' but around identification of interests which consumers in general feel to be appropriate. Thus they might involve users and ex-users of a variety of health and social services, together with their friends and supporters. As in decentralization, some degree of latitude in interpretation of centre policy would be necessary for its implementation to adapt to local influences which can only be an unknown factor at the beginning of the facilitating process. By definition, levels of prescribed output and organization of workload cannot be fixed in a local state structured to follow this course.

> Professionals have a choice between imposing 'appropriate' needs on their clients or attempting to break down the latters' 'deindividualisation' (e.g. as an unemployed person, as a schizophrenic etc.) and assisting 'real' needs to be collectively voiced.[27]

In the second form of Athenian democracy a more populist welfare framework is intended. All the people are to have a voice, which is to be operationalized through their individual consumption or purchasing decisions. This is a direction in which the 1991 NHS and Community Care reform is leading. In its first phase, it allows intermediaries, such as DHAs and general practitioners to make the purchases. These intermediaries are immediately faced with questions about how to distinguish consumer preferences from professional carers' judgements of need and of which, among them, to give most weight to.

But as was stated above, it must always be borne in mind that these models are ideal types. For on the one hand the Athenian type of behaviour might seem to be quite incompatible with local state obligations in law and electorally to majority, articulated, social interests. But on the other hand it is already operated by, for example, those professionals who have co-founded with users voluntary pressure groups, doffing their professional garb by night. In this sense professionals have already attempted to break down the norms of public discourse to bring on the clients of welfare who have suffered in silence.

Operationalizing this framework allows study of key questions about the closures of British mental hospitals. Would one find controlled authorities rationally closing the hospitals which they had been told were least fit to serve for the future – for instance on the grounds of extreme remoteness to districts served or lack of viability in terms of the relative decline of the resident population – and thus cases of rule book judgements? Would one encounter clinical opinion leaders in guided authorities designing innovations that would permit resettlement of the asylums residents and bidding for funds to support their development? As a third possibility, might closures be facilitated through mutual lobbying and adjustment of autarchic DHAs and correspondent agencies within the local organizational network – with a part incremental, part negotiated evolution of new services displacing the mental hospitals? Might DHA power sharing with voluntary organizations, consortia and other relevant interest groups, within decentralized bodies, be the key facilitator of plans for the replacement of the asylums? As a fifth more radical possibility, might consumers be empowered by the professional care givers of an athenian local state and seek to opt out of the traditional services – persuading providers or purchasers to contract for alternatives?

Table 1 Local responses to closure initiatives: ideal types of authority action (key features)

Controlled	Guided	Autarchic	Decentralized	Athenian
Authorities make decisions by reference to government instruction manuals.	Government gives incentives to professional product champions who bid for resources through their authorities.	Authorities take their services and resources into the health market, competing with and adjusting to the bids of other market leaders in order to respond to public pressure as consumer demand.	DHAs share decisions and provisions for health services development with outside agencies, and resist the temptation to predetermine agendas.	Consumers of care are supported by authorities either to form democratic organizations or to make informal 'purchasing' decisions which the authorities implement.

The government's 1983 de-hospitalization pilot programme, followed by Griffiths investigation into community care, could be seen as the beginning of central direction of mental health services. However, though Griffiths recommended the appointment of a Minister for Community Care, no such Minister was to be appointed. A central government directed devolution of large psychiatric hospital services to their catchment area communities was therefore an unlikely outcome.

Whether community health councils, and pressure groups such as MIND would be able to persuade individual health authorities to embark on reform programmes would of course depend on local circumstances. Certainly, in at least one of the case study districts, Islington, which will be discussed in Chapter 5, decentralization of local authority services under a socialist regime made for some civic similarity with the regions of Italy which received mental health reform most warmly. Moreover, once health authorities had been granted powers to 'buy in' services, then the question of the accountability to local publics of their purchasing decisions was raised. Adoption of an athenian model of action for closure initiatives was thus not out of the question.

References

1 Cooper, J.E. (1986). Professional obstacles to implementation and diffusion of innovative approaches to mental health care, Paper presented to a Conference held at the Center for Advanced Study in the Behavioral Sciences, Stanford, California, on 'Innovations in Mental Health Care Delivery in the U.S.A. and the U.K. Impediments and Implementation', 13–15 November, pp. 25–6.

2 Burrell, J. (1986). *The Psychiatric Hospital as a New Community*, London, Burrell Foley Associates.

3 Barrett, S. and Fudge, C. (eds) (1981). *Policy and Action*, London, Methuen.

4 Lindblom, C.E. (1965). *The Intelligence of Democracy*, New York, Free Press.

5 Marmor, T.R. (1986). *The Political and Economic Context of Mental Health Care in the US*, Paper presented to a Conference held at the Center for Advanced Study in the Behavioral Sciences, Stanford, California, on 'Innovations in Mental Health Care Delivery in the U.S.A. and the U.K. Impediments and Implementations', 13–15 December, p. 22.

6 Palmer, I. (1985). State theory and statutory authorities: points of convergence, *Sociology* 19: 4.

7 Ham, C.J. (1986). *Managing Health Services*, study no. 3, Bristol, School for Advanced Urban Studies.

8 Alford, R. (1975). *Health Care Politics*, Chicago, Ill. University of Chicago Press.

9 Bachrach, P. and Baratz, M.S. (1970). *Power and Poverty: Theory and Practice*, New York: Oxford University Press.

10 DHSS (1982). *Health Services Development: the NHS Planning System*, London, HMSO, paras 14–16.

11 National Institute for Social Work (1982). *Social Workers: Their Roles and Tasks*, Barclay Report, London, Bedford Square Press.
DHSS (1986). *Neighbourhood Nursing – A Focus for Care*, Cumberledge Report, London, HMSO.

12 Bulmer, M. (ed.) (1986). *Neighbours: The Work of Philip Abrams*, London, Unwin Hyman.

13 Robinson, F. and Abrams, P. (1977). *What We Know about the Neighbours*, Durham, University of Durham, Rowntree Research Unit.

14 Abrams, P., Abrams, S., Humphrey, R. and Snaith, R. (1981). *Creating Care in the Neighbourhood*, London, Neighbourhood Care Action Programme, p. x.

15 Cooke, P. (ed.) (1989). *Localities*, London, Unwin Hyman, p. 12.

16 Wilmott, P. (1986). *Social Networks, Informal Care and Public Policy*, London, Policy Studies Institute.

17 Higgins, J. (1989). Defining Community Care: Realities and myths, *Social Policy and Administration*, 23, 1.

18 Billis, D. (1984). *Welfare Bureaucracies*, London, Heinemann.

19 Glennerster, H., Korman, N., Marslen-Wilson, F. and Meredith, B. (1982). Social Planning, LSE mimeograph.

20 Centre for Corporate Strategy and Change (1989). *NHS Change Series*, published by Warwick Business School, University of Warwick.
21 Stocking, B. (1985). *Initiative and Inertia*, London, Nuffield Provincial Hospitals Trust.
22 Burns, T. and Stalker, G.M. (1961). *The Management of Innovation*, London, Tavistock.
23 Lindblom, C.E. (1959). Still muddling, not yet through. *Public Administration Review* 19: 2.
24 Benson, J.K. (1975). The interorganisational network as a political economy, *Administrative Science Quarterly* 20: 229–49.
25 Tomlinson, D. (1988). Let the mental hospitals close, *Policy and Politics* 16, 3: 187.
26 Bachrach, P. and Baratz, M.S. (1970). *Power and Poverty: Theory and Practice*, New York, Oxford University Press.
27 Tomlinson (1988): 186.

3

Britain 1986–9: the first big hospitals close

Powick

It was statistical analysis of trends in admissions to and discharges from mental hospitals that had led central government to plan for the redundancy of the hospitals. But the proposition that the trend of decline in the 1950s could be used as a baseline for planning in future years was much disputed. As Jones comments, 'possible variables such as the rate of development of community services, the aging of the population, economic uncertainty, and the limits of public tolerance, were mentioned, but were not weighted into the predictions'.[1] In fact the anticipated pace of rundown was not kept up and progress at replacing asylum care with general hospital treatment, as elsewhere in Europe, was slow. In 1968 the secretary of state drew attention to the fact that mental hospital services were 'lagging behind' the modern approach of DGH psychiatric departments and local authority community services.[2] The Department of Health decided to set up a development project to show how co-operative planning between hospital and local authorities could provide a comprehensive modern system of care. This was to focus especially on the apparent difficulties of resettling the mostly elderly long-stay population of the asylums. The area of Worcester was chosen for the development of a demonstration community service to replace the local mental hospital, Powick.

This was a centre initiative taken through a controlled authority. The fact that the long-stay population was not declining as rapidly as had been thought meant an expensive 'double running' situation. The new range of services would be supported alongside the old. The problem was therefore to find means of resettling a resident population apparently becoming more difficult to discharge. Local professionals had not been responsible for developing a closure programme and there is evidence that rehabilitation was inadequately co-ordinated prior to renewed efforts in the latter part of the demonstration programme. There does not appear to have been any significant pressure from voluntary organizations or the public. There was a cynical view that Powick was chosen as a government test centre after it was featured in a *World in Action* television report on overcrowding in psychiatric hospitals.[3]

Powick was built as the City and County Pauper Lunatic Asylum for Worcester in the mid-nineteenth century. In many ways attitudes and policies at the hospital appear to have followed a fairly typical course, with model behavioural regimes giving way to mass custody. In the first annual report of the medical superintendent it was reported that it had not been necessary to use the padded cell on any occasion, despite the fact that many patients had been admitted handcuffed, leg iron locked or bound with cords and chains. However, Wing suggests that Powick was noted in the early days chiefly for the cheapness of its care: 'The beauty of the setting and the amenities of the farm (510 acres) contrasted with the restrictive and pinchpenny regime.' He points out that according to the recollections of Dr Sandison, Deputy Superintendent from 1954 to 1964, it had been difficult to fill the beds at Powick with patients admitted from the county and that admissions from such places as Birmingham, outside the catchment area, often of severely disabled people, were accepted. 'Powick still had its reputation for cheapness and it made a profit.'[4]

Such warehousing was evidently mitigated by freedom from restraint. Gillard even considers that the hospital was in the vanguard of therapeutic optimism in the 1950s, 'being one of the first in the country to pull down the perimeter wall and unlock the wards, encouraging patients to mix freely'.[5]

The national plan for district general hospitals projected that Powick beds would be considerably reduced – from 1,089 in 1962 to 260 in 1975. But this in itself did not lead to Worcester being an obvious target for government to focus attention on, since such a reduction was in line with predictions for other hospitals. Probably the fact that it was, and is, an area of geographical averageness, made up of market and light industry towns dotted around a 'Middle England' farming countryside, played some part (though the area was well below average in relation to poverty, disease and social isolation). It was also thought that there was a very static population in the area which would be helpful to research into the efficacy of the new services. Results would be more reliable where there was only a small drift into or out of the area.

Interestingly the commercial value of the site did not play a part in the calculation. Despite long negotiations with the local authority planning department, the site did not figure in their 1982 County Plan for residential development and alternative health service uses were therefore being canvassed.

By 1975 the Worcester project was 'well under way', and by 1979 all the beds and hospital places, which were provided up to the prescribed national levels proportional to the catchment population, had been opened. The main service sites were at Kidderminster General Hospital and the Worcester County Infirmary, providing a combined total of 210 beds. A short-stay hostel was located at Kidderminster, with a long-stay hostel being provided at Worcester. Peripheral day hospitals and day centres were set up in Malvern and Evesham.

The administrative problems of phasing out Powick fell into three main areas. First, there was the state of the fabric of the hospital, and the cost of maintaining a satisfactory standard of accommodation in deteriorating buildings. Second, there was the difficulty of staffing the hospital to an adequate level, given that new entrants to the service were difficult to attract to an institution which was closing. The third group of problems related to the task of trying to rehabilitate the large number of elderly long-stay patients with intractable illnesses.

This last problem was clearly of greatest concern to government. As in many asylums, rehabilitation had tended to revolve around the acute admission wards from which patients were more likely to make a full recovery. This was reflected in the organization of the service within the hospital. As part of the effort to resettle the long-stay population the occupational and industrial therapy departments were integrated to offer 180 places specifically for this group. Further input was secured from consultant psychiatrists working in the new community units. They were to retain a commitment to sessional work at Powick, with the elderly population, under the reformed system. Finally, 'special attention was paid to staff training' in order to 'keep staff up to date, maintain interest and motivation'.[6]

It is evident from a Health Advisory Service (HAS) visit in 1985 that a fundamental flaw had been discovered in the planning of the Powick strategy. It had been assumed that increased rehabilitation input would achieve the 'big move' out of hospital and the restoration of substantial numbers of patients to some moderate state of well-being. It assumed that models of rehabilitation valuing people through work, which had been established at such hospitals at Netherne, could be applied for an indefinite period with all patients being potential benefactors.[7] These assumptions were to prove over-optimistic. Despite the increased input, remaining long-stay patients in Powick proved fairly intractable. It took much longer than expected for the population to be reduced by deaths, occasional discharges and transfers to new units.

By the end of 1978 when the new Powick replacement units were opened in the Worcester and Kidderminster areas, 343 patients remained in Powick. It proved difficult to discharge many of these patients. Thirty-one had been discharged by 1983 but with six of these patients having been transferred to a general hospital for physical illness and having subsequently died. 'With hindsight', the HAS commented, 'it can be seen that the exercise of moving to community care should have begun with the provision of substitute facilities for longer term dependent patients'.[8]

Despite the lack of recovery through rehabilitation the hospital population had been reduced to 189 patients in 1982. This was mostly accounted for by a 'natural' death-rate of 9 per cent per annum. But the picture was further complicated in 1983 when the Worcester DHA proposed to close another psychiatric hospital, with a similarly small and diminishing resident population, St Wulstan's, for which it had assumed responsibility. To achieve the closure the authority planned to transfer the remaining patients to Powick.[9]

Another problem which was uncovered during the planning process relates back to one of the variables which Jones suggested that government predictions had not taken fully into account. It had apparently been hoped that the numbers of long-term patients suffering from dementia would diminish with the rundown of the asylums. However, a contrary trend of rapid increase in the number of 'elderly severely mentally ill patients requiring hospital care' was discovered. In response, the Co-ordinating Committee for Powick, chaired by an academic from Birmingham University and involving six public authorities, decided to dedicate two further units specifically for this group, one being provided by the conversion of a general practitioner (GP) maternity unit.

What were the results of the Worcester Development Project?
Although Powick did not close until 1989, admissions had stopped a decade earlier. Lawrence, Cumella and Robertson analysed admissions to Kidderminster DGH during the first six years without the 'back-up' facility of admission to Powick.[10] They found that 'there was little or no accumulation of long-stay patients' during the period. Here then was apparent proof that the asylums were not necessary once the general hospital network was comprehensively developed. However, Lawrence and his colleagues caution that the lack of appearance of 'new long-stay' patients in the hospitals may have been due to geographical drift of such patients to other hospitals. In addition, a small number of people described as 'young organic patients' did become long stay but were transferred into the dementia unit at Kidderminster.

Between 1983 and 1986 Medical Research Council workers interviewed a large sample of clients at day centres and day hospitals in the Worcester catchment area.[11] The sample was made up of people whom they judged would probably have been long-stay residents of Powick if that option had continued to be available. The researchers identified 167 people who had been attending for a year or more. They were able to interview 139 of these service recipients, and in nearly all cases also interviewed their carers. Close relatives were questioned in approximately half of the cases. An interim report of the team suggests a reasonable degree of satisfaction with the new services with the majority of clients and carers viewing them as helpful. The social contact provided by the existence of the centres seem to be particularly valued. This had helped some to become more confident and others to feel less lonely.

Nevertheless a number of unmet needs were uncovered which are still the subject of analysis. Disappointingly there was little evidence of any change in the condition of attenders over the course of two years from the interviewing of the original sample.

One could argue on this evidence that the government demonstration had succeeded, subject to caveats about the need for caution in extrapolating from this study area possible effects on the rest of the country. Yet the problems of rehabilitating the largely elderly resident hospital populations remained unsolved. By the beginning of 1986, when alternative facilities were being planned for the combined residual population of both St Wulstan's and Powick, it had been recognized that

> As the vast majority of patients are elderly and have spent long periods in hospital, it is unrealistic to expect them to live independently or improve dramatically on discharge. It is essential that alternative accommodation should be very varied in type and support to give the greatest degree of independence to patients commensurate with their disabilities and to enable adjustments to be made in small steps.[12]

The evidence nationally regarding 'new long-stay' patients was equivocal, with the need for residential provision to be made for such patients being strongly contended outside Worcester. Moreover, the results of Lawrence's evaluation of admissions to the new service had not become available until 1987. In its objective of finding ways of rehabilitating the residual long-term inpatient population, the Development Project had a singular lack of success. The transfer of patients from St Wulstan's to Powick, in order to bring about the closure of the former hospital, which housed a preponderance of younger long-stay patients, was planned almost in spite of the Development Project.

Central government was thus not able to give clear guidance drawn from the Worcester case for hospital managing authorities in the rest of the country. Those authorities continued to be faced with the same issues of escalating costs and deteriorating quality of service within the institutions. By the 1980s many asylums had contracted to a size which was dwarf-life when compared with the vast acreages and Palladian pretensions of their heyday.

The story of St Wulstan's Hospital forms a fascinating footnote to the narrative of events at Powick, which illustrates that Worcester Health Authority was as much *locally* impelled to rationalize mental health services, as pushed to do so by the centre. In fact there was ample opportunity to achieve this objective. In 1982 Worcester district management team (DMT) considered that

> two mental hospitals [St Wulstan's and Powick] each catering for about 200 patients situated some nine miles apart in the same district can no longer be justified in the present economic climate.[13]

Lying to the south-west of Worcester city, St Wulstan's had not historically been used for mental health services. In 1961 it was reopened as a
hospital dedicated to specialist services for the rehabilitation of mentally
ill patients, to serve the whole of the West Midlands region. The aim of the
'new' hospital was in part to lessen overcrowding in the other twenty
mental hospitals of the region, from which referrals would be taken, and in
part to develop specialist methods of treatment for those who did not get
better under ordinary therapeutic regimes. St Wulstan's began with more
than 300 beds, though it was never entirely filled. After a review of its
operation in 1977 it became clear that only a proportion of patients referred
from the other hospitals were being successfully rehabilitated and that St
Wulstan's had become another long-stay hospital. Moreover, its existence
was completely at odds with the national trend for community care, since
patients who were referred were brought to a location quite remote from
the area in which they had lived. It is surprising that the work and evolution of the hospital was not in any way linked up with the Powick project:
first, because of the knowledge evidently acquired about the prospects and
techniques for resettling the long-stay population, with which the Department of Health was concerned, and second, because of the enhanced rehabilitation resources which it offered. At the time of its merger with
Powick, in the closing stages of the rundown of the latter hospital, the
fusing of specialisms was seen to offer many advantages, but by this time it
had already been decided to resettle residents in permanent community
hostels.

Banstead

Banstead Hospital, situated in the Surrey commuter belt, was the first large
hospital in Britain to close in August 1986. The closure was doubly important because the catchment area covered the inner London districts of
Westminster, Paddington and Hammersmith. The situation was radically
different from that obtaining at Powick. Whereas Lawrence and his colleagues had suggested that patients suffering from chronic schizophrenia
might have drifted away from Worcester and Kidderminster, one of the
major concerns about community services in London was that such patients tended to relocate in the inner city areas of the capital. These were
precisely the areas covered by Banstead. The population of this hospital
was double that of Powick, running to nearly 800 patients in 1979. The
very size would seem to militate against action on closure, with the point
of non-viability being some way off.

While the area health authority (AHA) had commissioned work to consider the future of its long-stay hospitals, the looming 1982 reorganization
of the NHS by which the area tier would be abolished, did
not augur well for any initiative to be taken forward from such work. The
easiest option for both district and area administrators would have been to

Figure 2 Location of: large mental hospitals serving London, case study district general hospitals, and the Haringey catchment areas, Tottenham and Edmonton

Notes:

	district health authority (DHA) boundaries
....	borough boundaries not coinciding with DHA
×	location of large mental hospitals serving London
+	district general hospital sites
WXH	Whipps Cross Hospital (Waltham Forest)
NMH	North Middlesex Hospital (main site for Haringey)
SAH	St Ann's Hospital (subsidiary site for Haringey)
WHH	Whittington Hospital (Islington)
TOTNAM	Tottenham
EDMNTN	Edmonton

Source: Mental Health Services in London, Greater London Council 1985.

do nothing until after the reorganization had taken place. The tradition of incrementalism was strongly established within the NHS and the tendency to avoid conflict was inherent to its administrative culture.

Why, then, was the Banstead strategy conceived so early? Paradoxically the threat to their survival posed by reorganization appears to have gingered up the interested members of the dying Kensington, Chelsea and Westminster area authority. 'Members knew about Jenkin's proposals and the removal of a tier in the NHS and sought a monument to their existence.'[14] Within the AHA ranks was an influential caucus of members which functioned in some ways like the group of the political party in power within a local authority. They met separately from the authority and shared a common 'soft Left' platform of views on the future of the NHS. Observers suggest that this group was very much one of its time: it played a role in the breakdown of the supposed post-war welfare consensus and in polarization of attitudes around more overtly political positions on state social policy. One member of the caucus was particularly prominent in its activity and was well known as an innovator in the NHS.

It was this group of AHA members which was responsible for the establishment of an Area working party on mental health services. The death of the AHA was not the last word of its members, since the caucus moved across to a position within the new Victoria District Authority, which took over responsibility for the management of the AHA's asylums. The caucus thus gave continuity at the top throughout the development of the closure plan. Pressure from this group was applied to prompt officers to take action when the momentum flagged. Such pressure was important, since it was apparent that some of the officers within Area Working Party were satisfied with the production of 'sliced bread statements': manifestos of intent which did not necessarily carry any promise of implementation.

The precipitating factors for the closure of Banstead were not different from those which applied elsewhere in the country. General hospital units were being developed within the catchment area of the hospital and its function as an admissions unit would eventually be superseded. In addition it was very remote from the catchment area, located fifteen miles from central London, representing a considerable journey given the density of the urban areas to be crossed and the paucity of public transport systems in Surrey.

But the story of closure cannot be told beyond this point without analysis of the other psychiatric hospital managed by the AHA with which its fate was so closely bound. Horton Hospital, located in Epsom, and together with Banstead one of a ring of mental hospitals in the vicinity known as the 'Epsom cluster', was subject to the same process of decline and was also in an impossible location to offer community care. Surprisingly given that it was chosen for closure, Banstead proved the more viable of the two hospitals in terms of admissions from the catchment area. It was Horton that was fast losing its supply of 'new entrants' with the opening of St

Charles Psychiatric Unit in Kensington, planned for 1984, being seen as a critical point. For Horton staff, particularly the medical staff, the loss of 'acute' (short stay) admissions would make the hospital a far less attractive place to work in. For clinicians who wanted to practise their skills and for nurses who needed the job satisfaction of returning patients to the community, there would be an uphill task with an entirely chronic and elderly population. Nurse education and training at Horton would be likely to become unsustainable without a sufficient variety of placements for students. The district management team 'feared that Horton would become very uncompetitive'.

From the point of view of cost-effectiveness and efficiency, it would have been surprising had the new Victoria Authority not taken an initiative. It had responsibility for two institutions within five miles of each other, both established for the same function and both less than half full. But the decision for closure had in any case already been made by the predecessor AHA.

The AHA working party had concluded in 1979 that there was 'no long term need for both these psychiatric hospitals to be retained to meet the service requirements of the area'.[15] The choice was between two options. The first was to run down both hospitals in parallel until a point of non-viability at either one of them was reached and a closure plan could be executed. The second was to close one hospital and transfer as many of its patients as possible into community facilities, resettling those who could not be so placed into the other, retained and upgraded hospital. It was this option which was chosen, and it was suggested that closure should probably take place when the combined population of the two hospitals dipped below the 1,000 mark. The management team of the North East District, said to be 'general management oriented before general management', was given the task of considering the details of closure and the strategy for transfer of patients.

To a historian of the health services this decision to rationalize the two hospitals on to one site could be seen as rather disappointing. For all the initiative, corporateness, political enthusiasm and managerial opportunism of planning for closure, it did not appear to bring in any noteworthy innovation. Indeed it could be argued that the AHA, and the North East District within it, was simply an efficient administration carrying out orders from the top. Banstead and Horton were both quite clearly remote from their catchment areas, and ill-fitted to serve in any future organization of local mental health services north of the Thames. It was therefore incumbent upon the AHA to plan alternative services. This duty was helped by the fact that the general hospital units being built up in the London catchment area were already taking over the functions of the asylums.

Yet the role of the caucus members and the DGM clearly lent a continuity to the lengthy process of planning closure which might otherwise easily have been lost. For his part, the DGM began by spending a day a week at Banstead from April 1980 and subsequently took six weeks off from running the affairs of district administration, handing over to his deputy in order to work full time on the strategy for closure. He became involved at a much more personal level, playing cricket at Horton. The only danger was, as he recalls, that he would have become institutionalized. Yet the DGM regarded the crucial administrative and managerial input to have been the appointment of a new Unit Administrator for Horton and Banstead in 1982. From that point on he only went down to the hospitals 'as and when required'.

The soft Left orientation of the caucus was also obviously important. The mental health charity MIND had already canvassed the idea of taking the opportunity presented by the decline in the population of the hospitals to argue for sale of parcels of land in order to fund community services. The problems for Kensington, Chelsea and Westminster to develop such services were manyfold. First, the authority was losing revenue resources to the outer London districts under the RAWP formula. Under the terms of this formula resources in the NHS were distributed in such a way as to favour areas of the country traditionally under-provided with services, such as the Trent region in the Midlands. Its application meant that London received a proportionally smaller increase in funding, year on year, than many of the Home Counties. This had a knock-on effect on capital resources, in the sense that they were taken up with developing general hospital services in the towns away from London. Second, the area was not fortunate enough to have been chosen for a government-supported demonstration project, despite the key issues of homelessness and health in the inner London areas served. Third, there was the added problem of the drift into the area from the rest of the country of patients with chronic illnesses. As was noted above, it was suspected that this was a factor in the lack of a build-up of long-stay patients in the new services established after Powick was closed to admissions.

In these circumstances the long-term future for mental health services in inner London was not good. Indeed a scenario of resources being drawn from the mental hospitals into the non-mental health budget might be readily anticipated. Heightened government concern with AIDS (acquired immune deficiency syndrome) and other 'new' epidemics, or with organizational change, might easily shift priorities away from the long-stay patient groups. By deciding upon a resettlement initiative at an early stage, the AHA was therefore making sure that its officers fully took advantage of the climate of growth for mental health services while it lasted. The release of revenue from Banstead was both to fund improvements at Horton and also to place the NHS elements of comprehensive district services inside the boundaries of the London district.

The strategy for Banstead could be seen in this light as an impressive gamble on resources for mental health being winnable within the region.

As the DGM was to relate shortly after closure had been achieved: 'Investment capital was the greatest difficulty [together with] the revenue consequences. We had no idea where the money was going to come from.' Underspendings from Kensington Chelsea and Westminster (on its demise) eventually provided a source for enabling the strategy to be implemented, and the regional health authority contributed £1.8 million as a loan from its Strategic Development Fund. This was to be repaid from savings of £7.5 million which were expected to accrue on the achievement of the closure. The Horton budget was to be increased from £10 million to more than £13 million for upgradings and improvements as the gradual transfer of patients from Banstead took place. These calculations allowed for £2.1 million to be made available for further community developments in Riverside to follow the closure (all these figures are given at 1986 prices). The breakdown is shown in Table 2.

To all appearances the AHA and DMT were responding to a *local* political environment which favoured the closure of asylums. At this stage the Left in politics was clearly interested in the development of alternatives to the asylums and this interest fed into the caucus policy-making. The concerns of what might be called the research and development agencies in the NHS, such as the Nuffield Foundation and the Kings Fund, also provided a stimulus for change. In this sense there was an element of autarchy in the planning of Kensington and Chelsea, responding to local market conditions. Enhancement of the NHS domain was certainly at the core of the initiative, perhaps because many informed observers thought that members of health authorities would, in the future, become both more representative of the population served and better able to make *local* management innovations in service.

Policy-making for Banstead clearly did not fulfil the autarchic ideal of mutual adjustment or joint planning between agencies to develop a pan-authority range of services. Initially at least, NHS resources were not being passed across to the local authorities and the voluntary organizations

Table 2 Budget for Banstead–Horton strategy

Revenue budget for Horton Hospital, incorporating service developments	£13,500,000
Reimbursement of Regional Strategic Development Fund for enabling schemes	£1,800,000
Revenue available for additional local service developments in Riverside	£2,165,000
Total	£17,465,000

Note: Figures derived from base budgets at 1 April 1986.
Source: Riverside Health Authority (1986). *Consultation Document on the Closure of Banstead Hospital, Sutton, Surrey*, London Riverside Health Authority.

active within the Riverside DHA which had by this stage succeeded Victoria DHA in another reorganization. This form of 're-provision' to achieve comprehensive services was not yet fully established in the thinking of the district management team: 'It was a debate that revolved around Kathleen Jones' (an academic expert on mental health services). The DMT was aware of the existence of the concept of a comprehensive inter-agency service, but knew that if they were to test the feasibility of implementing it, 'it would take an enormous amount of time'.

Nevertheless the hospital beds and places to be opened in London were seen as facilitating the further development of comprehensive community services. They were thus known by the name of 'enabling schemes'. As officers were to acknowledge in the formal consultation document on closure in 1986, community mental health services were not all in place in the Riverside District, but the underlying objective of the strategy, to release resources to fund community service developments, had been achieved.[16]

The negotiations that were taking place between the health authority and other organizations chiefly involved the other branches of the NHS. One such piece of negotiation offered clear proof of the way in which local rather than national forces were driving the change. In the analysis of strategic goals in the NHS in Chapter 1, it was noted that competitive tendering has been identified as an objective of the highest importance to central government. To managers of Banstead the policy was nothing but a hindrance and they felt that if the Department of Health insisted on the ancillary services of the hospital being offered to private tender, the process of counselling staff and keeping good industrial relations during the rundown would be railroaded. The path seemed otherwise smooth enough with a no-redundancy policy having been agreed. It would be bad enough for staff to deal with the problem of finding suitable alternative work within the NHS on the closure of Banstead. But to be faced with the short-term threat of redundancy at the hands of private contractors brought in by the health authority would mean that they might feel subject to a considerable degree of provocation. This raised the prospect of lengthy trade union conflict. The DGM thus argued for Banstead to be absolved from the competitive tendering process.

Here then, Victoria DHA was resisting the imposition of a cherished national policy in order to achieve its local ends. For the managers, if the case for absolution from competitive tendering were lost then the strategy for Banstead was rendered non-viable. After considerable local negotiation staff at Banstead agreed to accept the transfer of patients to Horton provided that managers did win the exemption from the requirement to go to tender. For their parts, the RHA and the DHSS, since they were already implicated in the Banstead–Horton plan, were unlikely to jeopardize it by opposing the local exemption requested. Indeed, the local strategists won approval for opting out of competitive tendering without having to approach the secretary of state.

In terms of crude numbers, the implementation of closure involved the transfer of around 350 long-stay and elderly patients from Banstead to upgraded wards in Horton. About 150 patients, the remainder inhabiting Banstead, would be transferred to community hospitals and hostels in London. The order of magnitude of these transfers suggests that problems of resettling the elderly long-stay population in the community were considered too daunting. Their solution was of course a key objective of the Powick project, which was still at an early operational stage in 1979. As was pointed out earlier government guidance was equivocal on the issue of whether the older generation of asylum residents could live successfully outside that environment.

In fact the local psychiatrists shared a firm conviction that the older generation of the long-stay population should not be moved into the community. This was an important judgement for management, who might otherwise be cast in the role of rationalizers whose goal was simply to move patients between wards and institutions as the needs of economy dictated. In the report of the DMT to the AHA in September 1980, which resulted from the intensive summer strategy exercise, one of the most significant paragraphs runs as follows:

> It has been widely accepted that it is in the interests of individual patients, that psychiatric treatment and services should be provided as near as is reasonably practicable to the patient's home and community. . . .
>
> When however consideration is given to which patients should be transferred back to locally based *hospitals* from the geographically remote major illness hospitals, there are comparatively few for whom such a transfer is in their best interests, clinically or socially.
>
> It is the advice of Consultant Psychiatrists at Banstead and Horton that while there may be a 'small number of patients in other categories who might be suitable on an individual basis for transfer to appropriate alternative facilities, there is only one category of patient which can seriously be considered for transfer. These are the patients being treated for dementia'.[17] (my emphasis)

This judgement sets Banstead and Horton within the historical frame. It was the first big closure to be actually implemented. In terms of local organizational interests, the twin principles of decanting to London hospitals on the one hand and to another large asylum on the other were not felt to be incompatible with modernization of the service. These principles were, however, to become the object of fierce criticism, especially as the final symbolic phase of the boarding up of the hospital was reached with its emotional leave-takings. What was significant about the Banstead strategy in this respect was that offering continued inpatient care to 'decantees' was presented by psychiatrists as a protection of patients' rights, particularly the right to stay in hospital where, they argued, 'many resist any suggestion that they should leave the hospital and also become more ill when such suggestions are made . . . *to press such a matter against the patients' will would certainly not be in their best interests'.*[18] (my emphasis)

Spotlights on the outcome

Towards the date for closure of Banstead, in mid-1986, two researchers from the national offices of MIND carried out a brief study of the closure process. This led to the publication of an extremely critical discussion document.[19] MIND's particular concern was the lack of a coherent strategy between the different health and local authorities which had been served by Banstead. In their view the recently created Riverside DHA which had become the managing agency, was interested only in providing hospital services and had paid scant, if any, attention to the need for a range of after-care facilities across the statutory and non-statutory sectors. The enabling schemes were seen as the beginning and end of community care. Finally MIND bitterly attacked what they believed to be the RHA's intention to cut the Riverside budget for mental health by 45 per cent.

The DHA responded to the MIND critique, strongly refuting the charge of having no coherent strategy and of not seeing beyond the enabling schemes. Nevertheless it was acknowledged that these did principally involve the creation of acute and continuing care NHS beds, with transfer of resources to local authorities for other schemes still being subject to further consideration. The DHA assured MIND that there were no plans to cut the mental illness budget, though there were issues about changes in the funding formula within the region for the very long-term future.[20] As the DGM was later to point out: 'The 45 per cent included the revenue which I had negotiated for transfer to other districts which had been dependent on Horton and Banstead. That was a part of the Horton and Banstead strategy and wholly consistent with its philosophy of local care.'[21]

But more criticisms were to follow, this time following evaluation of the Banstead outcome by the local Westminster branch of MIND, and a pressure group, the Coalition for Community Care.[22] They were chiefly concerned with the destiny of the £2.1 million identified within the strategy for community developments (Table 2). As they understood the position the RHA had stated since that this funding would have to be applied in the short term to supporting the development of acute admission beds at Charing Cross Hospital, to serve the residents of Hammersmith and Fulham. Had national MIND therefore been correct in their accusation that the enabling schemes actually represented the beginning and end of community care? The new RHA formula for funding district spending also came under scrutiny. It appeared that Riverside would be £3.1 million overspent on mental health services if the formula were to be rigorously adhered to.

While this analysis was being made against the background of a worsening position for NHS funding, it is difficult to determine whether the development moneys will be lost as the critics maintain. When I carried out a second interview with the DGM in 1989, the district was still arguing the case with the RHA for the £2.1 million (then uplifted to £2.5 million) to be made available.

Aside from the issue of funding beyond the enabling schemes, how were services in the catchment area working after the closure? Hatch and Nissel posed the question 'Is Community Care Working?' in a survey of care in Westminster, again carried out on behalf of the local branch of MIND, and published in October 1989.[23]

As a way of answering this question they studied a sample of 215 patients discharged from Westminster hospitals. Residents of the City of Westminster, while falling into the catchment areas of three different health districts, did not have recourse to admissions to any long-stay hospitals after the closure of Banstead in 1986. Hatch and Nissel felt that the outcome of the new style of service was particularly critical for 'new long-stay' patients, who, by their definitions while not continuously residing in hospitals, tended to be admitted at regular intervals for brief periods of treatment. They found that more than half their sample did have previous admissions within the preceding year. 'By looking at what happens after the long-stay hospitals have closed and at the fate of people who might in the past have found their way into such institutions', MIND argued, their survey 'offered a more exacting test of care in the community.'

The survey was somewhat equivocal in its findings. There were some notable gaps in care but on the whole the research can be considered reasonably reassuring, given the strongly critical stance toward the decision-making for Banstead which MIND's research officers had adopted.

On the positive side 'three in five of the sample were discharged into accommodation judged by staff to suit them well or to be at least satisfactory'. On a negative note, more than a quarter of the sample were homeless or of no fixed abode on admission to one of the Westminster hospitals, and the same proportion were homeless on discharge. This apparent failure to improve housing outcome is mitigated by the fact that a number of this group who were referred to the Homeless Persons Unit, together with others who went to Bed and Breakfast accommodation, would 'presumably in due course' have found their way to independent accommodation.

Where patients' views themselves were known, it was found that one-third of those placed in hostels would have preferred unshared, independent accommodation. On the other hand there was a divergence between staff judgements of need and the judgements of those discharged from their care, with staff opting more often for supported accommodation and the dischargees for independent living. Three in five were judged to need day care of some kind; for three-quarters of those needing it, day care was arranged.

For MIND itself, the outcome of the survey indicates that if community care has been established, it is not yet working:

The core health and social work services are made available. [But] the general picture of community care presented by this evidence on the fate of short stay patients following the closure of long stay hospitals is much more disquieting than the evidence on the planned discharge of long stay patients.[24]

Exeter

The difference between the closure process for the Exeter hospitals and those at Powick and Banstead is in one sense highly significant. In Exeter there was a considerable shift away from the mental hospital-to-general hospital model of change. This embraced new community mental health centres and the development of hostels for long-term clients in residential areas. The novelty of these services meant that the area, as a pioneer development centre, soon attracted visitors from all over the country.

However, other circumstances of the changes suggest that similar forces for change were at work to those elsewhere in the country: rationalization, the drive for cost-effectiveness and the redrawing of hospital catchment areas. Initial attempts at change came in the wake of the 1974 NHS reorganization, when efforts were made to sectorize Exminster, Digby and Wonford House Hospitals, which together made up one administrative unit as the 'Exe Vale Group'. Exminster and Digby had been built in the nineteenth century as the County and City lunatic asylums for Devon and Exeter. Wonford House was a smaller, more modern, hospital. The Exe Vale group served a largely rural area covering 2,000 square miles with a population of 600,000.

The fact that Exeter, in south-east Devon, was providing psychiatric inpatient care to the whole of the county, mostly based in two large hospitals, presented the worst kind of picture of mental health care, the very antithesis of care in the community. The position was grimmest at Exminster, the largest institution, which had housed more than 1,500 patients in its heyday, and still had more than 1,000 residents in 1972. A clinical decision had been made in the 1960s that this hospital should serve elderly people, while the other two hospitals would care for acute admissions and the 'chronic' long-stay population. As one analyst observed;

All the patients and staff had to look forward to at Exminster was death.[25]

After 1970 the Devon catchment area was split into four parts; the North, the South, Exeter West and Exeter East. However, neither this administrative change, nor the 1974 NHS reorganization, in themselves, brought about a more locality-oriented system of care. A reorganization committee was established for the thirty-nine wards of the three hospitals. But there were many problems to be faced. It was calculated that 80 per cent of patients would need to be moved between wards to achieve sectorization. It was not clear whether such moves would be to their benefit. A great deal of negotiation between sector teams would have to take place to bring about an equitable redistribution from the point of view of staff workload.

In 1979 an operational researcher was brought in from the academic world to look at the use being made of Exminster. His work revealed that the Exeter District was under-using the hospital, in so far as most patients were being admitted from the other districts in Devon. Clearly this insight enabled administrators to start thinking about whether, within Exeter at least, a different form of care was not more feasible. While the rising tide of the elderly population indicated that the need for inpatient care would not diminish, plans had already been made to establish local units for people with dementia at Tiverton and Exmouth. If the other Devon districts were in fact the chief suppliers of patients and users of the big hospital facilities then it would make sense for management and costs to be handed over to them. This logic gives a clue as to how the problems of sectorization and staffing were to be approached by Exeter managers. The general aim was to hand these problems over, if only at a conceptual level in the first instance, to the North and South Devon district management teams. In this strategy, however, like their counterparts in the North East District of Kensington and Chelsea, officers of the Exeter District would manage the handover. It was they who would decide upon an equitable redistribution of the hospital revenue which their district controlled. Exeter would act as principal negotiator with the other health authorities and the county social services department, and with the other health authorities, loaning some of its own senior managers to the latter agencies in order to ensure that they implemented change, so guaranteeing withdrawal from the big hospitals.

The opportunity to achieve a notional transfer of management responsibility to the districts, which were the heavy users of the institutions, was provided by the 1982 reorganization, through which North Devon and South Devon (Torbay) became autonomous districts. The Exeter district, now free from the shackles of the Devon area authority, could negotiate from a stronger management position with the 'receiver' districts. Two options were canvassed. The first was for Exeter's own services to be concentrated on Digby and Wonford House Hospitals, with Exminster to provide only for the other Devon districts. Alternatively, Exminster could remain as the hospital for elderly mentally ill patients, allowing a planned closure of Digby Hospital after short-stay beds had been established in Torbay and North Devon.

A decision was made in favour of the former option and again a similar trend of events to that in Banstead could be detected. Since Torbay and North Devon had developed very few local services and did not have the capacity to take back their patients from Exminster, some 'enablement' programme for such local services would have to be devised. A financial 'sweetener' was made available by the Exeter District to Torbay to help the latter to establish inpatient provision. This took the form of a gift of the proceeds from the sale of a hospital farm. This was a kind of down-payment toward the construction costs of a new psychiatric unit in Torbay General Hospital, which was to be known as the Edith Morgan Centre, after the founder of the 'Good Practices in Mental Health' organization.

Beyond this point, it is stretching credibility to make comparisons be-tween Banstead and Exeter. In Torbay adventurous changes were being proposed, with a focus of service on patch-based care around 'walk-in' community mental health centres. These were to be situated in ordinary houses in the main towns – Paignton, Totnes, Torquay and Newton Abbot. Although each patch would have a back-up long-term hostel, it was intend-ed that the mental health centres should take over the role of caring for most people with longer-term difficulties. An outreach team would pro-vide support to those living in independent accommodation. For elderly people assessment facilities were to be provided in each locality, with long-term care to be given in the private sector.

A further key difference between the South West and the Epsom cluster is that the advice of psychiatrists in the two areas pointed managers in opposite directions. While the planned closure of both Digby and Exmin-ster did mean some transitory inter-hospital transfers, both the chronic long-stay population and elderly people with dementia were considered to be better cared for in the community. To the non-expert this is an extraor-dinary state of affairs. At one institution a group of medical officers argued that it was against the interests of most long-term hospital residents with chronic illnesses to be resettled in community units. Indeed, those officers went even further, suggesting that the very promotion of the idea with such patients might lead to an exacerbation of their illness. At another institution this issue was apparently not even in contention.

In part this difference can be ascribed to the historical framework. Merger of Banstead and Horton had been decided upon as an option as early as 1979, and NHS managers were unsure of how far comprehensive community service without mental hospitals could be developed. There was particular caution where London was concerned since communities were less stable. Decision-making for the Exe Vale group came later on, around the time of the 1982 reorganization, when the debate about local services was no longer simply an academic one. But the difference also reflects the need for autarchy within district management teams in the NHS, which had to deal with uncertainty about patient outcomes within a vague set of government guidelines. There was a strong element of a gamble on the future in any psychiatric hospital closure. Central govern-ment was not prepared to take that gamble, but was happy to see the localities take it.

When looking at the local underbelly of the centre initiative at Powick, it was seen that the provision of more than one psychiatric hospital within a district, after 1982, meant certain death for one or other institution. In

Exeter, there were not two, but three, psychiatric hospitals. It would have been remarkable if no closures had been planned.

Two practical problems stand out above others in precipitating the predictable management action. The first stemmed from the arduous shift patterns worked by staff in Exminster in the late 1970s. For a number of reasons to do with the local labour market and domestic economies, staff clung to a twelve-hour shift system. This system made it difficult to provide sufficient cover to care for patients above safety or custodial observation levels. More intensive rehabilitation activities with chronic and elderly patients were ruled out. Many of these activities would involve staff escorting patients from the wards into the community for 'trials' in shopping, using buses, finding directions outside hospital, and so on. Escorts would require more overlap between shifts to allow staff to go off the ward. The twelve-hour shift pattern was also an obstacle to change in that it would have made it difficult to recruit new staff for hospital development. Having visited other long-stay institutions to make some notes about comparable conditions and arrangements, the district administrator was also concerned about the strain on staff imposed by such long hours. Such strain could easily kindle the kind of staff attitudes that had led to neglect of patients in some of the other large hospitals.

The second factor precipitating change was that Exminster, which consumed most of the resources, was expensive by any account both in terms of revenue and capital. Yet this expense seemed little justified. Professionals working in the service in the 1960s and 1970s spoke of poor conditions in the large dormitories with little personal space or privacy. In fact Devon appeared to be some way behind other areas of the country in the 1960s and 1970s. But if upgrading of all the wards were to be embarked upon it was evident that it would cost a small fortune. Nevertheless, the conditions obviously needed improving. It had cost £0.75 million to bring just one ward up to scratch. At £15,000 per annum per patient in 1982 the hospitals were 40 per cent more expensive in running costs than asylums at the cheaper end of the range. As the then district administrator put it, the district had scratched around for every spare penny over the years and sunk it into the hospital, and yet more and more resources were being demanded.

A crucial factor in achieving the change from hospital to community in Exeter was that district finance officers were able to fund their new services from within local budgets. This got over the critical problem of the 'double running' costs: the extra expenses of developing community services while having to support the infrastructure of the institution closing. The budget for Digby and Exminster was divided between the three districts concerned – Exeter, Torbay and Devon – in proportion to the respective RAWP rating of each. The implication of the formula was a major redistribution away from Exeter and toward the other two districts. This clearly provided a major incentive to the other two districts to achieve the development of new services.

The results: overexposure?

The biggest problems in the running of the new services after closure seemed to have been encountered in Torbay. However, expectations of a nirvana in mental health for visitors to the 'English Riviera' (as the area is promoted for tourist purposes) may have proved too great for some. The service was hailed as a pioneering advance in community care. Its four community mental health centres were modelled on experience in the USA and Europe. Indeed, this was one of the few areas in the early 1980s to be aware of the significance of these centres for early intervention in psychiatric illness, aimed at countering the drift of clients into inpatient facilities and dependency. A relatively small number of beds (per head of population) was planned at the DGH in recognition of this new development. While careful arrangements were made for the placement of every long-stay patient from Exminster, there was no direct reprovision of wards in the hospital as wards in the community.

After eighteen months of the new type of service, it came under strong attack, first in the Press and second from concerned professional observers. In June 1988 the *Torbay Herald Express* ran a largely complimentary story on the DGH unit, the Edith Morgan Centre (EMC), investigating why it had been 'thrust into the limelight . . . in a string of incidents involving patients treated at the much talked about psychiatric unit'. The death of a popular local singer had prompted a hunger strike by a friend over policies at the EMC. But allegations that patients were not given adequate care after they had been discharged from the unit were, on balance, in this investigation, unproven.[26]

Later in the year, according to the *Nursing Times*, a storm hit the unit. This began with

> South Devon Coroner Hamish Turner's comments on the fact that around half of the 32 people who had committed suicide in the area in the past year had, at some stage, been treated at the centre. Distressed relatives were soon telling the local press tales of how their depressed loved ones had managed to leave the unit just hours before their deaths. Nurses and their colleagues were quick to defend

Table 3 Mental health budgets in Exeter (1986)

District	Before (£m)	After (£m)	Change (%)
Torbay	2.6	4.6	+ 77
North Devon	1.3	1.8	+ 38
Exeter	8.0	5.5	– 31
Total	11.9	11.9	

Source: King, D. (1988). Replacing mental hospitals with better services, in S. Ramon (ed.) *Psychiatry in Transition*, London, Pluto, Table 17.1, p. 196.

themselves. During a meeting in which long-standing grievances were aired, staff shortages, poor communication with management and frustration with a badly designed building were highlighted. Nurses also pointed out that in the initial panic after Mr. Turner's remarks, the centre had been operating illegally by locking patients in the unit. Staff went into dispute with the Health Authority.[27]

Following this storm over the Coroner's remarks, the RHA asked an academic to carry out a short inquiry into the problem of suicides in Torbay.[28] The academic chosen, Professor Morgan of Bristol University, found no significant difference between the suicide rate in Torbay and that elsewhere in the country. Nor was there a difference in the proportion of those committing suicide who had previously been in touch with the psychiatric service. Nevertheless, Professor Morgan highlighted concern about whether there was an adequate number of both acute beds and long-term residental places. He was thus 'pleased to learn that consideration [had, at the time of his report] already been given to increasing the provision of residential facilities for patients with chronic illness'. Other issues were that the potential of the day hospital was not being fully exploited and that the mental health centres were evidently not properly integrated with the general hospital unit. Finally, Morgan commented that enormous demands were placed on the staff of the latter unit and recommended a review of its organization.

In 1988 Virginia Beardshaw of the Kings Fund, a charity promoting innovation in the NHS, and Edith Morgan, who had lent her name to the general hospital unit at Torquay, carried out a survey of the Torbay mental health services.[29] Like Professor Morgan before them, they were able to feel assured that the new service was working reasonably well. The development of the four community mental health centres (CMHCs), in particular, seemed to have been successful. At Culverhay, the first CMHC to be opened, at Paignton in 1984, an analysis of users suggested that a caseload representative of both long-term and short-term clients was emerging. A trend was nevertheless apparent for clients to form a 'younger group of people from more privileged socio-economic backgrounds than might be expected'.[30]

Some problems are reviewed in the survey which perhaps owe more to difficulties imposed by the local economic circumstances than to structural features of the mental health system. These relate principally to employment and accommodation. Unemployment was higher in Torbay than nationally and the DHA had provided few opportunities for work, most of its effort going into the operation of a light industrial unit at Newton Abbot. Despite the commercial success of this unit and the facility which it offered of training in a range of skills, places were limited and the site was inaccessible from the south of the district.

As already noted, Torbay DHA maintained back-up hostels for its localities, with a total of twenty-eight places available for people with long-term problems. Judged against government norms, this amount of residential provision can be considered relatively modest for a district with a population of 260,000. Beardshaw and Morgan note the particular problem which letting for the holiday season creates in this popular resort area. While winter lets are available in abundance, the coming of the spring means that tenants occupying these short lets have to move on. There are then severe shortages of accommodation for local people for the duration of the holiday season. While there is further assistance for mentally ill people from a local charity, the Parkview Society, which operates a hostel for ten people, 'the work of the Society is impeded by the lack of accommodation in and around Torquay, which means that its hostel places are frequently "blocked" for long periods'.[31]

Beardshaw and Morgan also draw attention to the accommodation problems for elderly people. Though the DHA has made good provision for assessment and diagnosis, accommodation for those requiring long-term care, which is provided primarily by the private sector, was found to be insufficient.[32]

While the Torbay service was unusual in its strong emphasis on mental health centres and movement away from residential centred provision, Exeter DHA adopted a more cautious attitude in the development of local services. Wonford House Hospital continued to be used for acute and rehabilitation services and though a mental health centre at Tiverton has been developed the schism between the old and the new has not been so marked. It is probably for this reason that Exeter services have not attracted the baleful glare of publicity.

Summary

The strategies adopted for the closures of Powick, Banstead and Exminster were at once puzzling in their diversity. At Powick the strongly centrist mode of operation meant that the health authority and local authority service framework adopted was built on assumptions about needs that were established wisdom (though whose, as was seen in Chapter 2, was not clear). Their relevance to Worcester itself, and to the Worcestershire towns of the 1980s was something which would have to be learned from experience. At Banstead, while similar centrist elements are present, the DHA was quite ready to contest national guidance. Not only was it, in Horton, recreating the age of the large mental hospital, but also it was seeking exemption from the DHSS requirement that health authorities put their ancillary services out to private tender. The strategy for the catchment area looked more than a little unstable, since revenue funding for services beyond the DGH units was not necessarily secure. In the case of Exminster this strategy was secure, but the rundown was barely comparable with those pursued at Powick and Banstead. Here there was no need for closure to hover behind the death-rate, or for one mental hospital to be engorged for another to shut. The revolutionary proposition was that all patients could live in community units outside the asylums, and that their placements could be funded from the revenue sunk into the big hospitals. It is no wonder that the service became a centre of attraction for all those with an interest in mental health. Nor is it surprising that the HAS, on their visit to Powick in 1985, recognized that the lack of a mass resettlement policy at the hospital was one of the demonstration project's principal shortcomings.

Though there were hints of autarchy within Kensington, Chelsea and Westminster AHA, and of a guided change at Exeter, the remoteness of these two asylums from their catchment areas and the obvious over-bedding which their maintenance entailed, fitted them snugly into government policy intentions. It is possible that local managers were looking over their shoulders in planning ahead; there was little pressure on them from the informed public to achieve rundown and disperse asylum services.

At all three locations there were elements of the themes in community care to which Knapp draws attention. Probably few of the most stout defenders of direct state welfare provision, once they were apprised of the costs and failings of the asylums in question, would have argued against strategies for their rationalization. Naturally the major proviso for such accord would be that the resources spent on the asylums be entirely re-distributed within modernized health services. In that sense the British policy context was not contentious.

None of the three schemes appears to have resulted in a worsening of service to mentally ill people. On the other hand the dramatic improvements which the revolutionary nature of the move would suggest are not in evidence. The questions posed by the existence of the asylums thus remained as unanswered at the end of these closures as they had been at the inception of their planning in 1978, when NETRHA officers too were also beginning the difficult task of addressing them. But the NETRHA story was a different one entirely.

References

1 Jones, K. (1987). Trends in the Organisation of Mental Health Services in Great Britain in the Past 25 Years, *International Journal of Mental Health*, Vol 16, 1–2: 94–107.
2 Gillard, R.E. (undated) *The Worcester Development Project*, Paper presented to a Training Conference of the NHS National Training Council Standing Committee on Management Education Training, on the theme of 'Bringing about Change in the Provision of Long Stay Services', p. 2.
3 ibid., p. 3.
4 Wing, J.K. and Bennett, ·C. (eds) (1988). *Long Term Care in the Worcester*

Development Project, London, unpublished report of the Medical Research Council Social Psychiatry Unit, p. 1.1.

5 Gillard (undated), p. 1.

6 ibid., p. 5.

7 Ekdawi, M.Y. (1972). The Netherne Resettlement Unit: results of ten years, *British Journal of Psychiatry* 155: 742–3.

8 Quoted in Wing and Bennett (1988), para 1.7.

9 Worcester and District Health Authority (1983). *Future Proposals for St Wulstan's Hospital, Malvern*, Worcester.

10 Lawrence, R.E., Cumella, S. and Robertson, J.A. (1988). Patterns of care in a district general hospital psychiatric department, *British Journal of Psychiatry* 152: 188–95.

11 Wing and Bennett (1988).

12 Worcester and District Health Authority (1986). *Provision of Alternative Facilities for Powick and St Wulstan's Patients*, Worcester, para 1.b.

13 Worcester and District Health Authority (1983). *The Transfer of St Wulstan's Hospital to the Powick Hospital Site: Report by the Feasibility Study Working Group*, Worcester, para 4.1.

14 Author's interview with David Knowles, district general manager, Riverside Health Authority, 10 March 1987.

15 Kensington Chelsea and Westminster Area Health Authority (1979). Report of the *Area Psychiatric Services Working Party* to the September meeting of the Authority, para 3.1.

16 Knowles, D.J. (1986). *Preface to Consultation Document on the Closure of Banstead Hospital*. London, Riverside Health Authority.

17 Kensington Chelsea and Westminster Area Health Authority (1979). paras 9.5 to 9.7.

18 para 9.13.

19 Reid, H. and Wiseman, A. (1986). *When the Talking has to Stop*, London, MIND Publications.

20 Dexter, M. (1986). *A Critique of the MIND Report by Harry Reid and Alban Wiseman*, London, Riverside Health Authority, Mental Health Unit.

21 Personal communication from David Knowles to the author, 24 October 1990.

22 Gregory, I. and Hatch, S. (1986). *Implications of the Closure of Banstead Hospital*, London, Coalition for Community Care and Westminster Association for Mental Health.

23 Hatch, S. and Nissel, C. (1989). *Is Community Care Working?*, London, Westminster Association for Mental Health.

24 Hatch and Nissel (1989), p. 17.

25 Quoted in an internal document of the Exeter District Health Authority.

26 *Herald Express*, 20 June 1988.

27 Seymour, J. (1990). A litany of complaints, *Nursing Times* 86, 5: 19.

28 Morgan, H.G. (1990). Press Conference at Torbay. 14 February, Bristol, University of Bristol, Department of Mental Health.

29 Beardshaw, V. and Morgan, E. (1990). *Community Care Works*, London, MIND Publications.

30 ibid., p. 32.

31 Thornicroft, G. and Bebbington, P. (1989). Deinstitutionalization – from hospital closure to service development, *British Journal of Psychiatry* 155: 742–3.

32 Beardshaw and Morgan (1990), p. 53.

4

Policy-making for the closure of asylums by the North East Thames Regional Health Authority

On 23 March 1983 the Prime Minister, Mrs Thatcher, wrote to the Minister of Health to say that she had 'spent nearly an hour seeing representatives of the Medical Committee and nursing staff at Friern Hospital' at her constituency surgery two weeks previously. She had discussed with those present

> the new policy with regard to the provision of services for the mentally ill, the projected closure of the Hospital and the terms upon which a Feasibility Study is to be prepared.

'Having seen this Hospital through many periods of difficulty', the Prime Minister continued, she could understand 'very well' the problem of staff morale that the representatives had raised. She asked whether someone from the DHSS could discuss the matter with members of the Hospital Medical Committee, concluding by stating her view that

> such reorganisations should be approached very carefully indeed, making sure that any new system is better than the old.

Why did the RHA decide to close Friern and Claybury?

There was no indication that the RHA was being forced into a hasty or precipitate move. Officers had undertaken a review of the policies in both mental illness and mental handicap in response to the 1975 White Paper and 1976 priority services recommendations.[1] But it had taken four years from the completion of that review for a decision to be made on the future of the RHA's six asylums.[2] As the regional medical officer (RMO) explained in an interview with the late Geoff Bromley:

> You see, DHSS is saying 75 things at once and they never resource any of them. It goes in one ear and out the other. I would honestly

say, and it may sound arrogant, that although the White Paper came out in 1975 and it was some sort of a landmark to point the way, we were never conscious here of any tremendous pressure or even really of any light pressure to reorientate our services to the Priority Services.[3]

There were may factors which contributed to the delay in completion of the RHA's review of its policies on mental hospitals. One problem was that the RHA needed to ensure that any mental illness initiative was not inequitable with respect to the other neglected client groups. Officers of all the Thames regional authorities were also heavily involved in the work of the London Health Planning Consortium, which was aiming to rationalize the numbers of acute (general medicine) beds in the capital. As the regional nursing officer (RNO) revealed:

In 1981 when I came to Region it wasn't our concern with the big psychiatric hospitals. It wasn't Friern that was engaging our atten-tion. . . . The complexity of the catchments was why we got involved.[4]

NETRHA officers felt vulnerable on the point that the priority groups should have been getting an increased share of the regional budget. They believed that mental illness was substantally underfunded in their region. However, in the late 1970s they stated quite categorically that they were not able to take an initiative on the priorities set down in national policy. This was because their programmes for investment of capital funds (i.e. funds for the construction of new facilities), to support which 'growth' revenue for the running costs was of course required, were completely taken up with the task of moving general medicine out of over-provided London to the under-provided hinterland of Essex. They were also busy in following the national NHS plan to put more money into primary care services. In discussing its Strategic Plan for the decade from 1978, NETRHA set down a number of unachievable objectives, as it was required to do by the DHSS. The first of these was

major capital investment in the development and improvement of the hospital component of the mental illness and mental handicap services following the recommendations of the health care policy groups.[5]

Instead, AHAs would be expected to put in appropriate bids for develop-ment. In fact 'enabling' strategies were already well under way at the area level, with general hospital departments of psychiatry being established in several of the districts. There appeared to be a much greater awareness of the possibilities and scope for change at the local levels.

The RHA's review was carried out by a small team of experts led by a psychiatrist and including a senior nurse and a senior social services rep-resentative. As events turned out the review was hampered by the illness of the latter member of the team. Some of the criticism which its recommendations attracted was due to the perception that it concentrated too much on medical and nursing issues. The Mezey Report (as the review became known after its principal author) suggested that cautious progress toward rationalization of mental hospital beds could be made to allow two of the six hospitals to close.[6] Such closures would hinge on three conditions. First, there would have to be sufficient interest in adopting a new style of service shown by staff working at whichever hospitals were chosen. Second, it was argued that a range of local services in the catchment areas of the two chosen hospitals would have to be created *before* any rundown programme was agreed. Third, the remaining four hospitals from the six were not to be closed but were to become centres of specialist services, such as forensic services, each serving a 'quadrant' of the region.

The first point is important because RHA officers were more concerned with devising an objective method for determining which of the hospitals should close. The choice was inevitably seen as God-given at the local level. With hindsight the RHA would have attempted to follow the advice of Mezey on this issue and would have sought, as far as possible, change from within the institutions rather than imposing it from without.

The second Mezey argument appeared to be somewhat unrealistic. Neither local CHCs – 'watchdog' bodies established in 1974 to protect the interests of health service consumers – nor national MIND felt that local services could be financed without some simultaneous land sales at the contracting hospitals.

The Mezey Report's general recommendations were accepted by the Redbridge and Waltham Forest AHA, whose officers had responsibility for management of two of the psychiatric hospitals, Goodmayes and Claybury. However, the authority felt them to be impractical to implement because of the assumptions about resources. They suggested that instead of closure, half of the site of two hospitals might be closed to finance local services. The hospital management team for Claybury rejected the idea of the quadrant hospital concept, since this could not tie in with the principle of community care.

The Waltham Forest CHC not only was in disagreement with Mezey but also questioned the length of time it had taken the RHA to make time for a discussion of the report (one year). This of course reflected the RHA's preoccupation with other matters. The CHC went on to point out that it had already carried out its own feasibility study on the potential for a psychiatric hospital closure in Redbridge and Waltham Forest.

This work had begun in May 1979, when the CHC, jointly with the Waltham Forest District Management Team, commissioned an independent consultant to assess the scope for merging Claybury and Goodmayes.[7] Gordon Best's study included analysis of inpatient statistics, revenue costs, the capital value of the institutions, trends in population rundown, projected costs of community services and the plans of the health authorities. A major focus was the problem of how to resource a strategy for new local services. Such a strategy had to begin from recognition that

> only a fraction of the capital and revenue resources tied up in existing institutions can, in practice, be redirected toward the provision of district or community services. Intrinsic in the idea of bringing about a shift in resources, therefore, is the assumption that community and district services must be made available before any major reduction in institutional care is implemented. In other words a capital outlay and revenue allocation will, by necessity, precede the recovery of any sums realised as a result of the reduction in long stay services.[8]

The fact that the two hospitals were less than three miles apart, that they had a combined acreage of 375 acres, that they were outmoded from the point of view of treatment, and that both had 'spare capacity' because of the continued decline in the long-stay population meant that there was much to be gained from merger. On top of these matters of fact, it was held that 'where appropriate, a substantial body of socio-clinical opinion' supported substituting community-based services for institutional care. 'Appropriate' was of course the key word here. Best went on to list conceptual and logistical barriers to achieving a merger.[9] The latter concerned the question of whether reliable estimates of the capital to be realized and of the costs of projected community services would be made. The former though, brought out once again the weak foundation in national policy for any large-scale resettlement of the long-stay population. 'Given that many patients in institutions such as Goodmayes and Claybury regard the hospital as their "home", will it be possible', asked Best, 'to identify that proportion of patients susceptible to, or likely to benefit from, community care?'[10]

Despite the many difficulties which would have to be faced in consolidating the hospitals only two of the twenty-four members of staff whom Best interviewed felt that there was little value in taking the study further: 'Rather the majority felt that the integration of Goodmayes and Claybury represented a tangible, largely desirable and far from impossible objective to achieve.'[11]

To conclude the report a programme for possible implementation was set out, which involved a development loan being made available to be repaid as the two institutions were rolled into one. The loan would fund both upgradings at the hospital to be retained and new community services. The scenario painted suggested that Claybury might realize as much as £25 million, with Goodmayes, like Horton after the closure of Banstead, becoming a hospital of around 1,000 beds.

Work was also going on independently among the main groups of professional care staffs to determine the future pattern of psychiatry within the area. A year after the Best assessment, the joint care planning team (JCPT) for Redbridge and Waltham Forest produced its final report. As in the rest of the region planned general hospital units, in this instance at Wanstead and the King George V sites, were the focus of the discussions. But the JCPT did not envisage any radical change flowing from the development of these units. Claybury would continue to serve for 'sub-regional specialties', while the team attached considerable importance to the monitoring of the effectiveness of rehabilitation at the general hospitals. Only a good monitoring system would allow judgements to be made about the possibility of moving long-stay patients out of the asylums on a large scale.

Nevertheless there was a central thread running through the JCPT report which linked it to the feasibility study of merger which the CHC had commissioned. It was proposed that land should be identified at both hospitals which could be released to fund new community services. One such innovation would be a pilot community mental health centre linked to a twenty-four-hour emergency psychiatric clinic at the general hospital for Waltham Forest district.

Within the Friern catchment area debate about the closure of the hospital was also widespread. In September 1980 a meeting of the local CHCs with members of the Camden and Islington AHA was told that the North Camden

> CHC had been saying for a long time, and it seemed to be falling on deaf ears that a date should be set for the closure of Friern and that money should not be spent on the hospital but on services in the community. Admissions should cease to Friern. DGH units should cater for acute work and long stay units should be established in the Districts.[12]

There was a crucial difference between the debates concerning Friern and Claybury. The future of Friern was being addressed by the top of the office. A small group of AHA members, in consultation with officers and the heads of professions, was attempting to develop a plan in line with the recommendations of national policy. The AHA had in fact been debating the issue of the future of the hospital for some years. Like the governors on hospital boards before them, their chief concern was to ensure that a scandal was not about to hit the hospital. They were rather like seismologists trying to detect the vulnerability of the hospital on an imaginary patient-neglect scale where the staff–patient ratio, amount of activity for patients, and the condition of the fabric had to be constantly monitored. In the late 1970s the AHA made significant efforts to determine a once-and-for-all decision for Friern. In response to the government's 1975 White Paper, they commissioned a small working party, led by a psychiatrist, to examine the potential for basing mental health services in the constituent districts and away from Friern. It is interesting that these were exactly the issues that Mezey was concerned with at the same time, though for the whole of the region rather than one area. One can speculate that if Mezey had not come up with the idea of dispensing with two hospitals, and of the remaining four being given a quadrant of the region to serve each, the idea that it was an *RHA* rather than *local* management responsibility to deal with the issue, might never have stuck in the minds of senior regional officers.

In a tour of only six weeks, the AHA working party concluded that the short-stay admission facilities of the new DGH units, then just established at the Whittington, Royal Free and University College Hospitals, were just about sufficient for the treatment in the catchment areas for the future. The main gap was in provision for elderly people with senile dementia and for the new long-stay population. Recommending how such provision could be made within the districts, Glancy (as the report was known after the psychiatrist leading the group) concluded that admissions to Friern could cease after the date when the proposed new services were in place.[13] This view tied in with that of Mezey. The scenario at this stage was that Friern would be allowed to die with dignity *à la* Powick, once the catchment district services were sufficiently strengthened to provide for all new patients. It was considered inhumane to move out the large number of 'old long-stay' residents who had been there for many years. Their lingering presence would thus save the hospital at least for the lifespan of the generation to which they belonged.

Despite the apparent gentleness of the Glancy approach to the sensitivities of staff at Friern, when the members of the authority attempted to work out a process for implementing its recommendations, they ran into considerable difficulties. Chiefly, they found that there was no professional consensus in the JCPT that all types of patients be provided for in the districts. After several meetings between the members and the JCPT it was decided that the hospital should not close but should offer specialist services, such as psychogeriatrics and academic research. This would be in addition to the plans to house the long-stay patients in new buildings on the periphery of the hospital site. As at Claybury the sub-regional resource centre option seemed to be coming to the fore, this time with high-level support.

Shortly after Glancy had reported in October 1977, the efforts of the Camden and Islington members to decide the future of Friern received a further impetus. Serious allegations of patient neglect and abuse were made in the *Sun* newspaper.[14] Jean Ritchie, one of the newspaper's reporters, gathered her evidence by taking a job as domestic assistant at Friern for a week. She asserted that patients were regularly drugged against their will, and that all patients on the ward where she worked were locked in. Further allegations were made anecdotally in a vivid and disturbing account.

Ritchie painted a number of scenes in the life of the ward:

IT1,1[Scene 1]
It's comedy hour. The nurses like a laugh at the patients' expense.

An old Russian lady who speaks five languages but most days doesn't speak at all has to endure nurses teasing an old man into kissing her, several times.

She didn't like it. Unable to speak, she moaned. It is a low repetitive moan that she keeps up for the rest of the afternoon.

[Scene 2]
A man about 50 wanders zombie like around the ward. He pees only every couple of days.

When he does the nurses stand around timing him. Twenty minutes is his record, I am told, as a stream runs half the length of the ward.

[Scene 3]
Harold scares me. Young, probably only about 40. Big. Usually naked.

First thing in the morning before the 'medicine' took its effect, he would prowl the ward, opening doors, locking me in a bathroom.

Staring straight ahead always.

Sitting naked in a chair with a book in his hands, flicking through the pages but staring ahead, his legs caked in his own excrement.

'Tie him in a wheelchair', a staff nurse told a young male student nurse.

Tying meant fastening him in with a feeding tray. Harold would stay there all day.

[Scene 4]
Food, good food, comes to the ward on hot trolleys. First pickings are made by the staff, who fill their own plates. They are forbidden by hospital rules to eat anything intended for patients.

Hospital authorities go to tremendous trouble to give patients food they like and can cope with.

One old lady seems to eat only roast beef. A small dish of it comes up for her every day.

She rarely gets it. One of the staff has it.

Peter Farrier, then hospital administrator, refuted the allegations commenting that the article contained 'many untruths, gross distortions of fact and lack of understanding of the care of the severely mentally ill'.[15] His strong defence was supported by authority members, convened in a small working party to investigate the allegations.

The impact of this episode upon the efforts to change the style of services for mentally ill patients is hard to conjecture. But another national newspaper, this time one of the 'qualities', the *Daily Telegraph*, also pitched into the Friern fray. An internal 1976 report on Friern by the regional health authority's own long-stay hospital monitoring team was leaked to the *Telegraph*. The newspaper's report of its contents constituted such a serious slur on professional care staff that a number of senior physicians at the hospital took legal action against the publishing company.[16]

So for both Claybury and Friern a considered process of local planning within the respective area health authorities was taking place in the late 1970s. The plans allowed not only for considerable retrenchment of the mental hospital facilities, but also for the possibility that resettling long-stay patients would prove difficult and that more modern on-site village-style accommodation might be required. Sub-regional specialties were strongly favoured by professional care staff if not by members or managers within the authorities. Neither hospital was sufficiently remote from its catchment area to warrant the intervention of the centre to impose closure. To understand why the RHA became involved and wanted to force the pace, it is necessary to turn back to examine the state of affairs which was inherited by the authority from the old metropolitan health board.

The outstanding fact of the position in 1974 was that the region had 6,000 beds within the six large hospitals, but serving a population of fewer than 4 million. This crude total amounted to a massive over-bedding in psychiatry. The recommendations in the White Paper of the following year (*Better Services for the Mentally Ill*) indicated that it should be the long-term aim of the RHA to axe at the very least one-third of this provision, even if no general hospital units at all were provided. But such units were being set up. AHAs planned for new departments of psychiatry to be operational in 1976 at Harlow (West Essex), Chase Farm (Enfield), University College (Bloomsbury), the Royal Free (Hampstead), the Whittington (Islington) and Basildon (Basildon and Thurrock). All except the latter unit meant some form of withdrawal from the use of acute admission facilities at either Claybury or Friern. Moreover, there would be considerable scope for a centrally planned scheme of retraction across the six hospitals, since it was estimated that there would be a 34–42 per cent reduction in the psychiatric hospital population by 1986.

If regional officers were to take more than a passing interest in this pattern of change the writing would have appeared to be on the wall, but as the comments of the regional medical and nursing officers cited above revealed, it was some time before their interest was kindled. By that stage, the work of Mezey had changed the picture of a comfortable evolution of mental health services in which it was seen as an area or district task to put forward plans for development of community services. By proposing the zone hospital concept to enable closures, Mezey was outlining a pan-regional rather than district-focused development of service. During the process of consultation on Mezey, regional officers were therefore becoming much more aware of the issues, the opportunities and the constraints.

While the position was clouded by the forthcoming abolition of the area health authorities, regional officers seemed to be forming a view that some areas, left to themselves, would not react in an appropriate way to the circumstances of rundown. The hospitals would be left to retrench naturally, while community services would remain patchy and slow to evolve. Institutional inertia and the lack of local interest in mental health services could mean that the opportunities of the period would be missed. In particular it was unlikely that resources for non-NHS facilities would be carved out from retrenchment savings. District planners and medical committees were more convinced of the importance of cure for mental illness at general hospitals with all the supposed technological advantages that they possessed. These pressures were doubly in evidence in the fashionable and renowned teaching hospital environments of the University College and the Royal Free Hospitals. Medical interest groups, within the teaching hospitals, including those of psychiatry, had traditionally exerted considerable influence over NHS policy-making. Their stature presented large institutional constraints to the framework for community treatment. Commenting at a later stage on the commonly held expectation that London should lead developments in medicine, the Hampstead DGM was able to report that the Royal Free had 'in many ways been very successful in maintaining and consolidating its position'.[17]

A sceptic at the RHA might thus have good reason to believe that aside from development of hospital units either in teaching hospitals or in other hospitals having a subaltern relation to them through training arrangements, not much else would happen to achieve the aims of the government's priority services strategy. The policy did represent a major challenge and the RHA was well aware that some authorities would be more able than others to make the change. Perhaps this was the main anxiety, and the main reason for the RHA taking a role in local decision-making. It was certainly the view of one senior member of the regional team of officers (RTO) that

> In the case of Camden and Islington, the authority did have good officers, and they did have the capacity to plan for a future district based provision. There were local initiatives coming through on planning for Friern. In fact we expected them to solve the problem for us. We knew on the other hand that Redbridge and Waltham Forest was not a competent authority and it could not have achieved this scale of planning.[18]

This is a significant insight, albeit that it may not have been shared by the main body of regional officers.

Clearly the RHA was also aware that everything was not well at Friern both from the report of its own monitoring group and from the publicity arising from the *Sun* and *Daily Telegraph* coverage. As the RNO put it, 'Friern had been on the rack'. The moment the hospital became the responsibility of the new Hampstead Health Authority, one of its senior officers began to canvass regional involvement in an initiative on closure. In so far as the RHA did feel *impelled* to act, the constant worry about shortages of staff and inadequacies of conditions at its mental hospitals, making neglect or abuse of patients more likely to occur, played a significant part in decision-making. But in addition, as the case of Exeter illustrated, the difficulty of containing the soaring running costs of a declining institution was an obvious concern.

The hypothesis of the asylum founders, that cure could be achieved through placement in a segregated and controlled environment, had been nullified many years before. Whether his comment is taken as a malapropism or a keen insight, the view of one charge nurse that the hospital had become 'an archival thing' was apposite. For many 'chronic' patients they could serve little purpose other than that of the tramping houses for vagrants. Few believed that they could be transformed to fulfil the goals of 'modern' care. The deep-seated place of asylums in the national psyche would be difficult to break out of. In the eyes of elderly people many NHS hospitals were still Poor Law institutions, since many had been built originally as workhouses and had not changed a great deal in appearance. The same applied to asylums.

NETRHA officers were quite open about the costs issue. The option of maintaining the hospitals for any significant strategic period was simply untenable. However, it would be wrong to dismiss the initiative on these grounds as primarily a money-saving device. Going back to the early thoughts of the RHA on the matter in the mid-1970s, it had been recognized that the reduction in the hospital populations meant that there would be competition for any savings between the hospitals themselves and district services. What the RHA was intending to do was to transfer the hospital budget to community services, with extra funds being made available to support the hospitals through the critical final stages of closure. Running costs were therefore not to be cut by NETRHA and indeed they were to be substantially increased. As was clear from the *district* initiative at Exminster the alternative strategy, a long-term programme of upgrading the asylum wards to modern standards, would hardly have been countenanced by the most avid, non-expert supporter of public spending.

The subjective impressions which RHA managers formed on their visit to the hospitals while they were deciding what to do about them has continually to be borne in mind. For instance the regional treasurer, who was given the Friern and Claybury brief while still a deputy, had 'a personal commitment, having visited the hospitals and realised the urgency of getting people out of these awful places'.

But on the issue of the moral imperative, the RHA had evidently felt sufficiently undisturbed by the 1976 report on Friern to exclude priority services schemes from its 1978 capital development programme.[19] Regional officers had lived for many years with successive waves of moral outrage about the scandalous conditions within the asylums. Whether and how that might lead to radical change of practice was another issue. It is therefore very difficult to come to the conclusion that by 1982 there was a moral imperative to close the hospitals. After all in Scotland, by contrast, the building of new asylums was being considered.[20]

How then did the RHA develop its plan for closure?

The regional team of officers began from the basepoint of the Mezey Report, but this left them with considerable policy problems to solve since the zone hospital concept was supported neither by the constituent health authorities of the region (the AHAs and the DMTs), nor by the community health councils. The RTO therefore felt it 'necessary to re-examine some of the basic premises, [and] to explore further the underlying assumptions before formulating specific policy proposals'.[21] As the regional medical officer explained:

> we had the Mezey report and the ideas about quadrants for mental illness hospitals. But the logic of the report was that we provide a two tier service [new general hospital wards, old asylum services]. We rejected this concept in consultation.
>
> There was then the general context, RAWP had been sorted out, our other strategy had to be priority care, and we had to fund geographical equity and care group equity.
>
> There was an in house enthusiasm for the closure policy and we then had the quasi objective choice of hospitals exercise [see Tables 4 and 5].[22]

After several years of policy development, the RHA came to the conclusion that it should aim for the closure of all the six mental hospitals, rather than just two. But since only a limited amount could be achieved within the overloaded RHA capital programme, it was decided to select two for a closure programme within the strategic planning period (1983 to 1993). This proposal was worked up within the broader terms of the long-promised priority care package. In July 1982 the RTO launched a consultative document in which the authority's four strategic priorities were listed as follows:

1 Implementation of plans for the development of local services for mentally handicapped people in the West Essex District, and the closure of Essex Hall.
2 Increasing the numbers of community psychiatric nurses.
3 Identifying districts for the development of comprehensive local mental illness services and making firm plans to provide these and facilitate the closure of two large hospitals, and providing local inpatient facilities for severely mentally ill elderly people.
4 Providing community nurses and local residential services for mentally handicapped people to accelerate the rundown of the large mental handicap hospitals.[23]

The estimated requirement for an increase in the resources devoted to priority services, which would be necessary to fund this strategy, was put at £10 million per annum in revenue terms and £62 million in capital. This amounted to 1.3 per cent of the RHA's annual revenue in 1981–2, and 'about seventeen months of its [then] current capital expenditure'. These global figures masked an estimated *decrease* in the revenue funding for mentally ill patients, for whom it was thought redeployment of the running costs of the hospitals to be closed would, in the long term, fund the new services. Compensating this apparent service cut for mentally ill patients was the fact that most of the capital to be set aside for the service developments would be devoted to building the replacement facilities in the community for the two psychiatric hospitals to close.

Accompanying the policy, the RTO put forward a 'Strategy for Action',[24] in which criteria for the selection of the two hospitals to be targeted for early closure were put forward. This 'quasi objective' exercise suggested that the RHA's need to sell the most valuable parts of its estate, in order to recoup the capital moneys advanced for the closures programme, was not its officers' primary consideration. The RHA's use of two of the criteria – service indicators and financial indicators – to arrive at a choice of hospitals is shown in Tables 4 and 5. The analysis not only compared the costs of the six hospitals, but also included the 'Yates' measure of the degree to

Table 4 Service provision indicators in rank order

Hospital/ factor	Yates's indices	Specialist facilities	Extent of local provision	Geo- graphical location	Coherence of catchment area
Friern	3	1	6	5	5
Warley	2	6	1	3	1
Severalls	1	1	1	1	2
Runwell	3	3	4	5	2
Claybury	6	5	5	3	6
Goodmayes	5	3	1	1	2

(Low priority for closure) 1   ⟵——⟶   6 (High priority for closure)

Source: NETRHA (1982). *The Future Provision of Services for the Mentally Ill: A Consultative Document.* London, North East Thames RHA.

Table 5 Financial indicators in rank order

Hospital/ factor	Total revenue expenditure	Trend of unit cost	Unit cost	Site value	Backlog main- tenance	Major upgradings planned
Friern	6	3	6	6	6	6
Warley	4	5	4	1	1	1
Severalls	3	6	5	4	1	1
Runwell	1	2	1	1	1	1
Claybury	5	4	3	1	1	1
Goodmayes	2	1	2	4	1	5

(Low priority for closure) 1   ⟵——⟶   6 (High priority for closure)

Source: NETRHA (1982). *The Future Provision of Services for the Mentally Ill: A Consultative Document.* London, North East Thames RHA.

which a mental hospital was considered to be 'at risk' because of poor staff–patient ratios, the geographical location of the hospitals relative to catchment area, and the comprehensiveness of local district provision (including social services facilities).

The RTO felt that the most important factor in any closure decision should be the extent to which local provision had been made in the catchment areas of the psychiatric hospitals. Judged on that basis, the analysis in the policy document suggested Friern as the best prospect and Claybury the second best. The RHA thus sought to 'encourage all those Districts which have an interest in a particular large hospital to come together to determine how the service can best be developed to meet local demands within the expected financial constraints'. At this stage regional officers had not yet committed themselves to any specific role in the implementation of the new policy. They did however state that there might be a 'Regional role in coordinating discussions at District level', owing to 'the special problems faced by Friern and Claybury with their relatively fragmented catchment areas'.

Nevertheless the keenness of regional officers on closure is clear from contemporary minutes of the RTO. At an informal meeting of the team in August the regional nursing officer spoke to a paper on consultation and implementation on priority services. She 'stressed the need for positive action on the proposed closure of two psychiatric hospitals, particularly because of the multi district dimension, which would require regional coordination and overview'. The regional medical officer spoke too of the importance of a 'firm coordinating role by the region'. It was agreed that regional staff of several disciplines would need to be seconded or appointed to 'spearhead the closures', while the routine meetings between the management teams of the region and the districts could be used to discuss details of implementation.

Consultation on the strategy was full indeed, with 2,600 copies of each of the care group documents issued. On the whole responses were supportive of the new strategy. The regional administrator was able to report to the RHA at the end of the consultation period in November 1982 that 'there had not been much opposition to the proposed closures'. None of the bodies consulted came forward with any alternative suggestions and

> of particular note was the positive acceptance of Waltham Forest district towards a local mental illness service and the eventual closure of Claybury Hospital.

Hampstead District had not made a formal response within the RHA's consultative period, but it was noted that

> Friern Hospital have stressed the importance of their supra district services and the need for a medium secure unit as well as provision for the special needs of long stay patients.[25]

In fact staff at Friern produced a lengthy critique of the RHA policy, while 'important reservations' had been expressed by other respondents. These concerned finance, time-scale, the need for asylum, dependence on the ability of local authorities to develop services, and the criteria for selection of the two hospitals for closure.

The RHA felt that it had sufficient grounds for proceeding with the initiative, and it was proposed to make 'one or more senior appointments . . . with specific responsibility for coordinating plans and ensuring implementation'. But in the light of the reservations of respondents, the RNO suggested that feasibility studies be set up to examine more closely the planning issues to be resolved for the closure of Friern and Claybury. These studies were to be carried out collaboratively between regional and district officers, and to be completed within six months, to minimize the uncertainty for staff at the two hospitals.

What were the results of the feasibility studies?

A clear consensus emerged that 'reprovision' of the two asylums by resettlement of the resident population was feasible, but not within the cost constraints set out by the RHA. Disbelief that closures could be achieved within these constraints was never to be wholly suspended and in important ways served to hamper the subsequent implementation process.

In their report of the feasibility work, the RHA's officers concluded that substantial rundown was going to happen with or without regional intervention.[26] The then current trends suggested a further 60 per cent reduction in the long-stay population within ten years. A lot of patient moves within Friern and Claybury would take place anyway as a result of ward mergers and relocation in line with continuing retrenchment. It had already been proposed to institute a new RHA funding policy by which the budgets of the long-stay hospitals were to be distributed between the district authorities served by them. Once implemented, this system would also give an added incentive to these districts to redeploy the funding for locally managed alternative care and treatment.

> The fact is that the RHA cannot sensibly opt to do nothing. The processes that have been described will go on in any event. The real question is whether the changes – which affect the psychiatric provision of half the districts in the region – should be properly planned; or whether the RHA is prepared, as an impassive bystander, merely to observe them.[27]

There was a further undercurrent of anxiety were major intervention not to be made. The decade ahead was one in which it was projected that there would be no growth in the Department of Health and Social Security's annual allocation to the NETRHA. The demographic and technology pressures on the NHS would make it difficult to maintain the then existing level of service across the specialties. The RHA could foresee only a worsening of the position on mental health. This was firmly stated in the report of the closure feasibility studies which was produced for public consultation.

> Given the present economic constraints on the NHS it is inevitable that there will be reductions in the present level of resources tied up in these two hospitals.[28]

There did not appear to be any certainty that the RHA would make capital gain out of the exercise, whether or not such gain might be applied for non-mental health purposes. As a result of the feasibility studies, regional officers were now prepared to make £50 million capital funding available. Payback remained very much of a hypothetical order. The Friern site did not have planning permission for development, the frontage of the hospital was a listed building, and large areas were zoned for public open space by the planning authority. Claybury lay in the Green Belt around London and therefore money-generating residential or industrial development on any large scale was proscribed. Decisions were being taken well before the British property boom of the 1980s.

Like all other public authorities, the RHA followed the negotiating norms by which new developments were planned in the NHS. In this instance DHAs had begun the process in their feasibility reports by putting in 'bids' for resources which were couched in ideal terms. The expectation was that the RHA would respond with substantial pruning – whether of staffing or building costs. DHAs would then try to achieve a lesser level of pruning, and the RHA would consider that position. By this means the usual order of events led toward a compromise solution eventually being reached. But this often took years to achieve, and in the case of Friern and Claybury, the whole process was being telescoped into a period of months.

It was because of these expectations about planning that members of the RTO felt they could comfortably cut down on DHA estimates of the revenue required for community services. This was so even though the DHAs wanted twice as much revenue as was then being spent on the large hospitals. In an internal RTO memo the comment was made that

> It must be remembered that districts have not really given an 'in depth' consideration to the respective functional briefs [for proposed reprovision projects]. This is not their fault but entirely due to the speed with which the programme has had to move to meet the RHA target date. We are, therefore, dealing with last minute ideas and on reflection I am sure that districts would be the first to agree that their desirable costings could suffer refinement without loss of function.

On the capital side, this meant that instead of all residential units being costed as if they would be 'new build', twenty-five of them could be sited in existing buildings. Even so, all developments were to be costed as if the

NHS would be the sole funding agent and that no local authority or housing corporation money would come in. On the revenue side it meant such
devices as changing the weighting of the staff mix so that a greater proportion of unqualified staff were employed than might ideally have been desired. On the other hand an increase in the amount of revenue funding was
now being proposed by the RTO, of the order of 10 per cent. During their
policy work on Mezey, NETRHA officers had initially thought they were
significantly underspending on mental health. This judgement was made
by comparing the percentage of the regional budget devoted to this service
with the corresponding percentages in other regions. But in fact, when
comparative levels of spending per head of population were studied by the
regional treasurer, it was found that NETRHA spending was more or less
right. As the RMO commented:

> The result of our review [of funding], contrary to my expectations
> was that we were *not underresourced* for Mental Illness Services. It
> showed that, allowing for double running costs, [there was] *more*
> revenue for Mental Illness Services than in fact we needed in com-
> parison with the White Paper benchmarks. This was a big surprise to
> us, and indeed, in some respects rather embarrassing. It looked as
> though we might have been cooking the books.[29] (my emphasis)

This finding naturally gave the RTO some confidence in dealing with the
arguments of the Claybury and Friern districts that they needed very large
increases in revenue to fund community replacement services.

Although the RTO felt strongly that it could not stand by, nevertheless
its members *could* have opted to do nothing. What was surprising in some
ways was that the RHA did decide to act. That the moral imperative was
not a sufficient condition has already been remarked upon. Overall this
seemed to be the case with the financial imperative too. For eight years at
least, the RHA had been considering simply shifting resources to the community as the natural retraction of the hospitals allowed. One option that
had been canvassed was for staffing ratios and care standards merely to be
maintained rather than improved as the hospitals declined. By pursuing
such a policy, ward closures could steadily release recurring funding for
redeployment elsewhere. Why not follow such a course given the controversy about the issue of district services being autonomous from mental
hospitals? There was clearly increasing competition for resources between
the DGH sector and the psychiatric hospital sector. But what was lacking
to underpin a choice between the two was agreement among clinicians
about which groups of patients could be treated and/or cared for successfully outside the asylum.

There was a problem about the diminishing proportion of savings from
ward closures as the hospitals got smaller, but here the RHA had every
reason to leave the issue for provider and receiver districts to sort out
between them. Redbridge and Waltham Forest had accepted that there

would be no major increase in revenue to fund the development of new services before closure and would plan on the basis that half of the sites of two hospitals could be sold to finance the new services.

Was the RHA aware of the conclusions of the Camden and Islington working party on Friern, that there should be new buildings for the old long-stay population on the Friern site, and that the hospital should be developed as a specialist psychogeriatric and teaching service? Were they aware of the Waltham Forest District and CHC view that merger of Claybury and Goodmayes was a feasible way forward? While individual officers may indeed have been aware of this work, consideration of it did not form part of the policy-making. As far as the RMO was concerned the regional authority was starting from scratch and had to ask 'How do you create a policy and on what do you base it?'[30] There were no 'off-the-shelf' prototypes to work towards other than the DGH cure focused service with all the faults already commented on. Major problems might lie ahead for the 'enabling' health service schemes, if they were not complemented by new local authority back-up services. The effect of removing the non-health housing and caring functions of the institutions had not been quantified. In short, it was not clear what would happen to the warehousing process once the warehouses had been removed.

As the RNO observed

> Nobody had planned a mental illness service before. There wasn't much fundamental discussion about it. The idea that the chronically ill could live in a domestic setting with little professional nursing input was new. Whereas mental handicap had revolutionized fairly quickly, for Friern and Claybury we were breaking this ground before the consensus had been reached.[31]

All that the RHA could offer were statements of intent about the desirability of building 'comprehensive joint health and social services for mental illness'. The details of how such intentions could be realized would be left to local joint planning and financing at the district level: 'any proposal to move the balance of care from hospital to community should come from the local level'.

The other major problem the region faced in trying to put together a strategy was that neither of the managing districts was actually convinced that it was feasible to provide a service completely devolved from the large hospitals. Hamstead inherited specialist hospital ambitions for Friern. Waltham Forest strongly contested the belief that modest revenue increases would be sufficient for reprovision of Claybury.

Perhaps most important of all, the RHA was not anticipating that there would be any serious opposition to the proposal to rundown the asylums. The responses to the first consultation document on the proposal on the contrary indicated that constituent authorities were very much in favour.

The idea of the feasibility studies was to clear three problem areas: to determine what kind of after-care provision the DHAs wanted to fund to complement DGH facilities, what kinds of models of service they wanted to achieve, and on the basis of this work to clarify whether district authorities did see asylum replacement as feasible or not.

The feasibility studies were very hastily carried out, however, and financial assumptions which district planners were working on were unclear. None of the districts came out with a clear resolution of the underlying planning difficulties, and the clear cut *local* decision in favour of closures which the RHA had hoped for, was not forthcoming. The general view of DHA planners was that new services would be far more expensive than those of the asylums, and that the funding the RHA was willing to put forward would be inadequate. This qualification of support for the replacement of Friern and Claybury meant that it fell back upon regional officers, once again, to decide whether to go ahead with the initiative, or to abandon it.

In an interview after she had left the RHA in 1986, the RNO vividly captured the way in which the pressure of the moment was telling on her team:

> Three years ago in that very hot summer the RTO spent a week locked in anguished debate. I don't think I'd ever felt so taxed in my career. So much of the costings depended on our estimates of nurse staffing. In the end I said what is the alternative [to closure] going to be? . . .
>
> I searched my conscience. With £50m capital we could surely produce something; prevent patients becoming as dependent. . . .[32]

The RMO shared her conviction just as strongly:

> We were keen to do right by the priority groups. We were keen that a comprehensive district based service must be provided. Friern and Claybury was thus our starting point and we thought we could surely provide something better than that.[33]

So the NETRHA decided to carry on with the Friern and Claybury programme in the absence of feasible alternatives. But officers were then immediately faced with the problem of how to implement the decision through DHAs not convinced that it could be done. In the words of the RNO 'It was the right decision, but it was a vale of tears.'

References

1 DHSS (1975). *Better Services for the Mentally Ill*, London, HMSO.
2 Fairey, M.J. (1982). *Consultation on Policies for the Priority Care Groups*, London, North East Thames Regional Health Authority.
3 Bromley, G.L. (1984). Hospital closure: death of institutional psychiatry? University of Essex, unpublished dissertation, MA in Social Services Planning, p. 54.

4 Interview with the author, 17 July 1986.
5 NETRHA (1980). *Regional Strategic Plan 1978–1988*. Section C.6, para 3, London, North East Thames RHA.
6 NETRHA (1980). *The Mental Illness Service in NETRHA: A Policy Group Report*, Mezey Report, London, North East Thames RHA.
7 G. Best in association with Brewer Smith and Brewer Maxwell for Waltham Forest District CHC (1979). *Promoting Mental Health in Redbridge and Waltham Forest: A Preliminary Study of the Feasibility of Integrating Goodmayes and Claybury Hospitals*, London, Waltham Forest CHC.
8 ibid., pp. 3–4.
9 ibid., pp. 16–19.
10 ibid., p. 16.
11 ibid., p. 19.
12 Meeting of Joint CHCs with Members Group for Psychiatry of Camden and Islington AHA, 24 September 1980.
13 Camden and Islington Area Health Authority (1977). *Report of an Area Working Party on the Future Provision of Psychiatric Services*, Glancy Report, London, Camden and Islington AHA.
14 *Sun* 12 January 1978.
15 ibid.
16 *Barnet Press* 12 May 1978.
17 Hampstead Health Authority (1985). *Griffiths Report – Implementation Proposals*, pp. 6–7, London, Hampstead HA.
18 Paul Walker (Regional Medical Officer) interview with author, 26 March 1985.
19 *Barnet Press* 12 May 1978.
20 Scottish Home and Health Department (1989). *Mental Hospitals in Focus*, Edinburgh, HMSO.
21 NETRHA (1982). *The Future Provision of Services for the Mentally Ill: A Consultative Document*, London, North East Thames RHA.
22 Paul Walker interview, 26 March 1985.
23 Fairey (1982).
24 NETRHA (1982). Part II.
25 Report to the RHA (1982). *Consultative Policy Documents on the Priority Services' Response to Consultation*, item 9, meeting of the NETRHA, November, para 4.4.
26 NETRHA (1983). *Report to the Regional Health Authority on Mental Illness Services in the Catchment Areas of Claybury and Friern Hospitals*, para 65, London, North East Thames RHA.
27 ibid., para 65.4.
28 ibid., para 49.
29 Bromley (1984). p. 45.
30 Paul Walker interview, 26 March 1985.
31 Interview with author, 17 July 1986.
32 ibid.
33 Paul Walker interview, 26 March 1985.

5

The response to closure from the localities: Islington, Waltham Forest and Haringey

This chapter outlines the decisions made by the key local actors in three of the nine health districts affected by the proposed closures. Islington and Haringey were chosen for in-depth study at an early stage in the research process since they appeared to be adopting models of reprovision which radically differed from each other. Waltham Forest was chosen as a third district for study when the author took up post in order that the impact of organizational and political differences between districts in the catchment areas could be assessed. This choice also meant that a balance could be struck in considering events at Friern and Claybury, with one district located in each catchment area and a third served partially by Friern and partially by Claybury.

The difficulty faced by the RHA in devising a mental health policy, it often seemed from scratch to its senior officers, has been made much of in the previous chapter. Policies for mental health have not been a focus of concern for central government beyond the need to rationalize beds to take account of the continuing process of rundown in the long-stay populations. There is clearly a great degree of action space for local professional care staff to exploit the conditions for change created by the rundown process.

In its deliberations after Mezey, there appeared to be two principles which the RHA would consider paramount. The first was that general hospital departments of psychiatry be established in the districts. The second was that a 'two-tier' service with rump asylums running alongside the DGH units should not be allowed to develop. Yet it appeared that even these two principles could be subject to adjustment. The regional medical officer could not have cared if it had been decided to keep 400 beds at a new Friern. In some ways, the RHA reneged on its own commitment to closure. Under the auspices of Hampstead as the 'provider' DHA managing Friern, it had been agreed with Haringey DHA during the feasibility studies, that one of the newer buildings on the site of the asylum – Halliwick House –

could be retained. This was to serve for short-stay patients from the western part of Haringey, whose psychiatrists had apparently long held ambitions to take it over from the other Friern 'user' authorities for such a purpose. In addition Hampstead intended to allow for specialist services (such as for patients with brain damage) to be provided to several districts around the hospital. This proposal, accepted by the RHA, was a return on a modest scale to the plans for the hospital which the Camden and Islington AHA had put forward before its dissolution. Only the determination of the regional nursing officer to resist a new large institution emerging led the RTO to impose a ceiling of 200 beds on the part of the site to be retained.

The regional treasurer was later to suggest that if a similar case for a remaindered Claybury had been put forward with the charismatic leadership which had come to the fore at Friern, the RHA would certainly have listened to the argument. But the same push and leadership for achieving that kind of prospect for the future was lacking from the negotiations. However, Waltham Forest, as managing DHA, was to reject publicly the RHA proposition that closure could be achieved largely within the revenue resources then spent on Claybury. The July 1983 decision of the RHA to go ahead was therefore in the teeth of local opposition on that side of the region. This led to serious concern within the RTO about whether the districts could be kept in line. But already events were moving rapidly on to the Griffiths reorganization and away from the Friern and Claybury focus. The RNO, designated leader of the reprovision exercise, could barely get 'the lowest of the low' to minute meetings. The plan to keep a firm co-ordinating role was dropped. An RTO sub-group of officers from different disciplines was established to take the work forward. In practice its efforts devolved to two or three members. They had the greatest difficulty in obtaining sufficiently detailed project proposals from district officers to enable them to begin dispersing capital funding for reprovision. This gave rise to an anxiety about whether the closure initiative was actually happening at the local level or not. Might it be railroaded by new central directives such as the general management reorganization, which was coming the way of the priority groups' initiative?

To a certain extent the RHA had laid the ground itself for this slow start to reprovision, since the capital to be made available was to be phased in gradually (see Table 6).[1]

It was felt that because services of this kind had not been planned before, it would take a couple of years for schemes to be worked out, especially given the dense committee structures of professionals that would seek involvement.

If the retention under a new disguise of both hospitals was hypothetically possible, what were the other options?

At the other end of the spectrum were attempts to withdraw from hospital-centred services and to focus 'entry' to treatment and care at community mental health centres. Crisis intervention would be offered as

Table 6 Phasing of capital expenditure
for reprovision

Period	£m
1985/86	1.25
1986/87	6.00
1987/88	10.00
1988/89	9.00
1989/90	9.00
1990/91	7.50
1991/92	7.25

Source: NETRHA (1983). *Report to the Regional
Health Authority on Feasibility Studies on Mental Illness Services in the Catchment Areas of
Claybury and Friern Hospitals,* Appendix D, p.
14, London, NETRHA.

a domiciliary service by which professional staff would visit and even stay
with clients undergoing crisis. Refuge houses rather than wards or nursing
homes would back up the new style of service. These ideas drew some of
their rationale from the changes in practices of social work which had
taken place in the 1970s. Professional intermediaries would activate, as far
as possible, 'natural' social support which individuals had through family
and friends in the community. They would try not to take over or to
substitute for this natural system.

Given the range of ideas involved, it was clearly possible that in theory
local pressures could determine a large part of the retreat from Claybury
and Friern. An intense debate was being conducted about the practicability
of the mental health centres. They did become a firm part of the plans of
both Haringey and Islington. Waltham Forest had already established a
pilot mental health centre and intended to evaluate its operation with a
view to extending the service. Nevertheless, on the whole, medical and
nursing staff were not convinced of the benefits of such ways of working
and tended to view the centres with some suspicion, taking account of
their apparent failure to provide long term support services in the USA.
Planners and administrators were more enamoured of the centres, but they
had few champions among professional care staff themselves.

No rigorous study of European or American experience was undertaken
but it was well known that these centres had tended to move 'up-market'
toward the articulate and 'improveable' users and away from the chronic
intractable dependants. Fears that this might happen did not lead to the
widespread abandonment of the concept, however. Rather the search was
on for ways to prevent the move up-market. It was an exciting time in
mental health. The opportunities were obviously greatest where the small
network of informed mental health lobbyists, often drawn not only from

among enthusiasts active in such organizations as MIND and Good Practices in Mental Health, but also from generic voluntary organizations, was
at its most extensive. Users' groups were just beginning to be heard of in
the distance, from The Netherlands and the USA. Later, after the planning
process was well advanced, they were able to exert some small influence
on plans in the Friern and Claybury areas.

These discussions have to be set in the context of the inner-city catchment area for which change was being proposed. The problems of community development which Thomas has identified, existed in abundance,
the principal one being a lack of civic competence. Residents lacked the
time, skills and motivation to take 'self-help' forms of action to protect or
enhance the quality of life of their area. Concern about health issues had
not, generally speaking, captured the local imagination, except through
campaigns to stop the closure of popular local hospitals such as cottage and
maternity hospitals. In two of the districts studied here the public profile
of the DHAs was dominated by the centralization of general medical services on the DGH. This meant the closure of a number of popular smaller
hospitals against bitter and well-supported local opposition. The position
in the other district was different only in that the process of centralization
was already well established by the onset of this study.

Bromley suggests that Haringey DHA, on its inception in 1982, inherited
'a major situation concerning the Acute services' which stemmed from its
position as a RAWP loser unable to fund priority services growth without
cutting acute general medicine. This led to a proposal to close one of the
three acute hospitals serving the district, the Prince of Wales, in 1979.

> When the matter formally went out to consultation during 1979, it
> produced substantial local adverse reaction, not least because the
> Prince of Wales Hospital, created at the turn of the century, com-
> manded much local support. It was small, local and for very many
> persons in Tottenham and East Haringey represented their major
> hospital. . . . The Community Health Council together with many
> other bodies, including the Local Authority, opposed the closure of
> the Prince of Wales Hospital and the accompanying reduction in
> Acute beds.[2]

In 1981 the under-secretary for state visited the district and stated that no
further action on the closure should take place until after further examination and consultation. Despite the local authority's subsequently employ-
ing a researcher to investigate alternatives, the Goverment finally agreed
to the DHA's plans for closure in 1983.

In Waltham Forest the DHA made proposals for the closure of two local
hospitals. This was in response to the same situation on acute services as
faced Haringey – over-provision on RAWP indices.

At their meeting in December 1983, when considering Operational Plan
proposals for 1984 to 1987, the members of the authority took the unusual

step of rejecting the officers' plans. Members were particularly concerned at the level of public protest against the proposed closures. The district administrator tabled a petition against the closure of one of them, the Jubilee Hospital, containing 11,345 signatures. A second petition against the closure of the other hospital, the Forest Hospital, had 4,500 signatories.

The policy for mental hospital closures was not subject to such opposition. In part this was due to the fact they had originally been sited well away from centres of population. They were meant to be self-sufficient communities, deliberately isolated from the general population. Thus they were not readily identified as 'belonging' to the local communities which had built up around them. In any case they offered a service to a relatively unpopular group of long-term NHS dependants. As long as relocation of the patients did not mean relocation in the middle of prime residential areas, concern took the form of a somewhat generalized fear of the consequences of closures. This was mediated by acceptance in the abstract of the civil rights of the mentally ill; rights which meant having the opportunity to live in a 'normal' community environment. Finally, the voluntary organizations active in this area, MIND and the National Schizophrenia Fellowship were divided about whether the hospitals should go. The NSF, while not positively favouring mental hospitals, felt that village-type settlements in plenty of space would be important if genuine asylum was to be available for those long-stay patients who needed it in the future.[3]

While there was the appearance of a large amount of discretion, the picture is a complex one, in which a number of factors worked to restrict the freedom of movement. DHAs were well equipped to build hospitals. While land was scarce in London, the rationalization of acute medical services and the movement of the majority of them on to one main district site meant that the outlying hospital sites became available for priority services. Central government guidance of 1980 indicated that the vacated cottage hospitals would be suitable for the treatment of elderly mentally ill people. Thus two factors, the school of *hospital* building in which DHAs had been educated, and the evacuation of prime development land in DHA ownership, bounded the more feasible options for reprovision of the early years. The odds favoured face-lifting of the vacated outlying general hospitals in order to provide accommodation for those displaced from the mental hospitals.

Buying 'ordinary housing' which would be suitable for group living, estimating likely costs of refurbishment, and gauging property value against the abstract yet valued qualities of 'community-ness' in any residential area, were not tasks for health service officers to undertake lightly. When they did begin to set about them, they were immediately faced with estate agents who preferred to sell to family buyers as sale to the DHAs would run rather than take the risk that prices of other properties in the vicinity might fall as a result of the establishment of something so potentially threatening to neighbourhood tranquillity as a group home for mentally ill people – with or without staff living in.

Like local authority housing departments, DHAs were also at this time being encouraged not to act as direct providers of housing. As the small hospitals in the districts were closed, staff housing was not necessarily replaced at the DGH. A number of nursing homes which had formerly served for staff at the smaller hospitals therefore also became available for community care. Here too were 'sites looking for a client group', as one Haringey planner saw it.

Finally there was the question of redeploying the nursing staff from Friern and Claybury. The ordinary processes of turnover and retirement from service would lessen the number of staff to be 'reprovided' over the ten-year programme. A staff transfer policy for each hospital involved counselling of staff in all departments about their preferred choices of employment in the new community services. In the case of Banstead and Exeter, no-redundancy policies had been agreed. At Powick the hospital was to be allowed to rundown naturally and therefore the problem of transfer was not so acute. For Friern and Claybury the DHAs did not offer a no-redundancy policy. Given that the closures had been imposed by the RHA, staff relations became a major issue for the reprovision process, with DHAs eventually giving a commitment to employ all those staff who were willing to commit themselves to work in the new services.

Local NHS managers had frequent recourse to what Bachrach and Baratz call symbolic normative values.[4] These had a strong patriarchal element, often found in medicine. At the level of treatment practices, DHAs would ultimately have to be guided by those with legal responsibility, the clinicians. The disposition of both staff and patients in a new service could, following this logic, be derived from their views. Another normative value was the responsible management of public money. This the apolitical DHAs could achieve, behaving impartially, balancing different interests and keeping to a predictable disposition of the budget. Local authorities on the other hand could be viewed as partial, factional and inconsistent in their investment of public funds. Despite the fact that local authorities, voluntary organizations and the housing associations were all funded by public money, the implication was that they were not quite so responsible as DHAs.

The vocational ownership of patients by the DHAs was another part of the symbolism influencing decision-making. Many of the medical and nursing staff had given long years of service to care in the psychiatric hospital. Their representatives strongly felt a moral obligation to continue to supervise care once patients had moved to the community. This need came out in several ways. Attempts were made by senior nurses to influence the practices of care in non-NHS projects. The case register approach to long-term care (used to keep in touch with all those suffering chronic illness in a catchment area) could be, and was, perceived as another controlling clinical intervention, coming after the fact of the transfer of responsibility for patients from hospital consultant psychiatrists to general practitioners.

Islington: autarchy within limits

In Islington these normative values were to prove especially important, inhibiting trends towards a redistribution of care and a lessening of the DHA's institutional dominance. Fashionable and subject to early gentrification, the London Borough of Islington (LBI) was perhaps best known nationally as one of the 'socialist republics' of Britain's inner city areas. The LBI was one of the first municipalities to promote gay rights and to attempt to counteract racism in its services and among its workforce. After Walsall, the LBI was in the vanguard of neighbourhood decentralization. The devolution of housing and social services functions to neighbourhoods was a key political goal which tended to thrust others into the shade. This radicalism produced its own reaction, however: a well-publicized Social Democratic party (SDP) coup among the ruling Labour party group of councillors in 1981. But the new SDP council which resulted was not to survive long, being roundly defeated in the elections in the following year, when the Labour group swept back to power.

For the Islington Health Authority (IHA) this kind of environment was one which was unwelcome. Its officers were quite frank about the impact on their work of a 'solidly left-wing' council. As one of them argued, it tended 'to make sensible planning rather difficult when there's a framework of no cuts and no rate capping'. Of the councillors appointed to the health authority itself, one was described as being rather more 'sensible' in planning terms, but in consequence thought to be alienated from the other left-wing members. DHA officers described themselves on the other hand as 'not political' but 'looking at what it is possible to achieve in practical terms within the resources'.

From the officers' point of view, collaboration with the local authority was thus fraught with political problems. None the less a free-thinking and faintly radical caucus of members running the DHA could be identified whose left of centre political sympathies were well known. The chairman himself was a former Labour MP who had left the party. Another prominent member had played a leading role in the defection of Labour councillors to the SDP that had caused control of the Islington council to change in 1981. The centrist political backgrounds of these authority members however, in their very moderation, added fuel to potential conflict with the avowedly left-wing Labour council. Some officers, though, had clearly made a positive choice of the environment of Islington in their NHS career moves, because of the opportunities for municipal planning which it offered.

Like the majority of the district authorities involved, Islington welcomed the closure initiative of the NETRHA but initially put a rather cautious interpretation upon its meaning for the area: it was seen largely to mean the building up of hospital-centred sevices around the DGH, the Whittington. A two-stage plan was produced from the feasibility study for closure. The first part would involve moving all patients to the

Whittington site. The second part would follow assessment of, and work with, the patients moved to the DGH. Those judged able enough would be resettled again, probably in non-NHS facilities around the borough.

The plan for a 'mass decant' from Friern to the Whittington fell in line with the programme for development of the general hospital estate through which the new district authority was coming of age. There were four district sites on which general hospital medicine was practised, which had been inherited from two distinct hospital management groups. As part of planned centralization on to three sites, DHA officers felt there to be important advantages in devoting the fourth vacated site to long-stay care.

> the Highgate site, which is agreed as a more desirable area for long stay accommodation, would be available for the development of mental illness services consequent on the closure of Friern. Such a scheme would be accompanied by new monies and capital invest-ment from the Region.[5]

Priority services were not just being given leftovers reflecting lack of pub-lic pressure on their behalf. The reorganization of general medicine in Islington on to three sites was expected to release recurring revenue sav-ings of about £0.5 million per annum. These savings were reserved for funding priority services development. The Friern initiative provided an opportunity for this strategy to be implemented in favour of the mentally ill. Aside from the bounty of the fourth site and the funding though, im-portant as these were, little could be detected of Islington-specific priorities coming to the fore. The Camden and Islington AHA had intended for several years to set up local facilities for the client group labelled the 'elderly with dementia' as a priority, and they had first claim to the DGH long-stay site. But even here, as the CHC was later to contend with vigour, there was little that was attractive about the proposed location to carers of elderly people in the borough.

Like the other districts, the Islington Health Authority was encouraged by the RHA to make more imaginative proposals. It was rather being reluctantly pushed out toward the autarchic reaches of public participation in policy-making by the centre. In the words of the regional nurse planner (RNP) at the RHA:

> Why propose two moves – 1, for the health services and 2, to the local authority? Let us take a 'giant leap for mankind' in one go.

Politics aside, it was surprising that the DHA had hesitated to exploit the potential scope for reprovision offered by LBI's commitment to democratic municipalism. Working in the borough were well-established voluntary groups providing facilities for ex-offenders, people discharged from both mental handicap and mental illness hospitals, and such special services as psychotherapy for ethnic minorities. Most of these groups received at least some of their financial backing from the council. In fact the LBI wanted plans to take a very different shape, but within the few months afforded to its officers by the feasibility study, they had hardly enough time to work out a position statement on a possible role for the council. The DHA had in any case assigned the council to a place in the second phase of moves away from the initial placement of patients at the Whittington. The council was merely invited to say what it might contribute to this order of events.

But NHS officers and professional carers also had fundamental misgivings about the propriety of any collaborative endeavour with the LBI. The biggest obstacle for the health authority was the apparent lack of prudence which the LBI, as its potential partner in the reprovision initiative, exhibited in budget setting. The council was at this time investigating the possibility of borrowing from financial institutions in order to maintain a level of spending no longer supported by central government. This was part of a planned resistance to pressure from Whitehall for public spending restraint. As the leader, Margaret Hodge, explained, the 'most important device' in this strategy was

> 'capitalising expenditure' – that is redefining current spending to take it off the rate fund or housing account and recording it instead as capital spending. At first, this capitalisation was funded from reserves, special funds or capital receipts (from enforced council house sales). But these sources of cash soon dried up and 'deferred purchase agreements' (DPAs) have been widely used instead. Under these agreements private companies, set up by merchant banks and other City institutions, finance some of a Council's capital spending, but defer repayments of capital and interest for a number of years. . . .
>
> By 1989–90, the deferred purchase agreements begin to run out and the spending will have to be absorbed back into local budgets. We shall also have to start paying the deferred interest charges. This would be an intolerable burden for local budgets and rates.[6]

There was the distinct possibility that the council would become non-viable. Councillors were in effect mortgaging the future of services. Their hope was that a Labour government would be returned at the next general election (1987) and lift the restraints of rate-capping. For the DHA in these circumstances, collaboration with the council could be something of a speculative endeavour.

The RHA's concerns were far removed from the political pedantry of Islington, since they also had to take account of the views of Conservative-controlled councils outside the inner London districts. But 'by exception', officers and members did hold discussions with councillors from Haringey, Camden and Islington during the feasibility studies for Friern closure. The RHA was keen to encourage the kind of idealized collaborative endeavour with the borough councils set out from 1974 in DHSS Circulars.[7] Its officers appeared to have far-sighted and liberal views. They recognized that *all* reprovision would have to be funded in entirety from the NHS, given the difficulties in which borough councils had been placed by public spending restraint.

As an arm of the centre, the RHA had to have the wider aim in view of 'pump-priming' the non-NHS agencies to achieve community care support systems. Given a lack of community care development over the many years in which it had been a national aim, this local authority and voluntary sector function clearly had a first call on any funds released from the institutions. But this RHA line was not without dissenters among regional officers. The Islington proposals to purchase local authority sites were the first of their kind to be considered by the RTO Friern and Claybury group early in 1985. They were the occasion for a heated debate among its members, who were well aware of the bigger centre–locality control issues. That the NHS should buy land and property from the council and then, on top of that, fund the council to run Friern reprovision schemes at the purchased sites was a particularly controversial idea. Nursing advisers in particular were not enthusiastic. For one of them it

'really ran against the grain',

while for another, RHA agreement to the DHA proposals would mean

'the first political purchase ever made'.

The regional treasurer, however, was firm in insisting that the RHA had to understand the position of the local authorities if it wanted their cooperation. He was aware of Hodge's problem – that any income received from the NHS for the social services to run Friern schemes in property remaining in council ownership would become subject to the controls of rate-capping. He also knew that the DHA was protected by the provisions of the government's *Care in the Community* Circular.[8] Once bought, the properties could not be used for another purpose by the council unless repurchased from the DHA at the full market price.

While the RHA was willing to cede resources and part of a care domain traditionally belonging to the NHS in this way, the picture was different at the local level. NHS officers recognized that they had to collaborate with the council but were visibly uncomfortable inhabiting this political environment. For once accepting the LBI's sale conditions they were, in a sense, taking part in the council's deferred purchase strategy. They did not have the option of saying: 'LBI's prospects are poor, therefore we need to look for another municipal organization as partner.' In a 'market' situation this is what they would have been able to do. But naturally, there was only one set of town hall departments gatekeeping the key assets of housing which were on offer.

Once the feasibility studies were over and 'planning for real' began, the DHA was able to assess in a more considered way how it might pursue the organizational interests associated with Friern reprovision. Within a 'joint' planning team in which, as was usually the case in the NHS, the DHA's own officers made up a majority, social services and voluntary sector organizations were nevertheless assigned a major role in the sub-groups on housing and preventive services. Taking the route already laid out by the RHA the leading participants, a consultant psychiatrist who acted as chair, the district treasurer, the district medical officer, the district works officer and the assistant district administrator, formed a high-ranking team working closely with the authority members' planning and finance group. With this foundation, the decisions of the planning team had a corporate strength which enabled the DHA to consider strategies for autarchy from the centre.

There was an element of farce about some of the buildings offered by the council to the DHA for refurbishment at NHS cost to house Friern patients. One of these, already in a dilapidated state, literally fell down after the offer had been made. Another was badly damaged by fire. As the secretary of the planning team commented:

> We have got to be careful as a health authority about the tendency of the Local Authority to offload what are really pretty poor properties onto us as part of the planning. Clearly it would be unrealistic and the sites are not available for new build, but that means that we can't be too optimistic about the phasing out of the running costs element [for building maintenance] which was such a huge part of the Friern revenue.

Nevertheless, housing was at least being made available. A housing association was also interested in buying one of the DHA's redundant and cleared hospital sites to provide housing for its own clientele which would include a number of dwellings for Friern patients. One of the voluntary organizations, the Peter Bedford Trust, was prepared to resettle thirty patients from the hospital. Two other voluntary groups, MIND and the Psychiatric Rehabilitation Association (PRA), came forward with proposals for reprovision group homes to be established in houses which they already had available and which could be adapted for Friern schemes.

There was much interest within the planning team in community mental health centres, and it was planned to establish three in the district. The principal psychologist in the DHA, who had experience of such centres from the USA, chaired a working party to produce a detailed policy for their operation in Islington. A nursing officer and planning officer subsequently posed as a married couple to tour estate agents' offices looking for suitable sites for a centre!

As it turned out, NHS officers on the planning team did not believe that there were thirty Friern patients motivated enough for the rehabilitation work of the Peter Bedford Trust. But they were prepared to accept a more modest scheme for a smaller group. This was the beginning of a period of considerable adjustment by the DHA to the other agencies in the network. The medical and nursing interest were prepared to relinquish some of the vocational ownership and to cede some of the NHS client group domain, confident that they could, in principle, retain financial control over the development and maintenance of the alternative schemes.

The LBI was a relatively good provider of mental health services, comparing favourably with other borough councils. Three day centres were run by the social services department and an after-care hostel. Adult fostering schemes were also offered, though it proved difficult to find suitable carers within the borough boundaries. The Finsbury neighbourhood in the south of the borough was the forcing ground for one of the very few 'local' responses to the Friern closure. This followed a discussion of the planned replacement of the hospital at a regular semi-formal lunch meeting of Church, voluntary organization and social services workers in the area. Those present decided they wanted to do something for the Friern closure. They approached local tenants' associations to seek their involvement in practical resettlement projects.

Whatever the priority being given to decentralization, mental health was something alive and well in the committee structure of the council. It was through this structure that the informed and concerned agencies involved with the issue tended to put their best efforts. There was a sub-committee of social services formed specifically to consider mental health services. In 1985, when the DHA engaged in formal public consultation on its proposals for Friern reprovision, this committee ran on after 11 p.m. in spirited debate of the contents. As one of the social services officers observed, this level of interest was extremely valuable.

It so happened that the committee was chaired, during the period from 1984 to 1986, by the councillor who was the key figure in decentralization. He had worked in mental health services and considered himself 'more than an intelligent layman' in these matters. Of course his input coloured the political environment still further, and provided something of an organizing focus for change agents. It was clear that he 'upped the ante' in officer relations between the two authorities. As one member of the DHA district management team put it describing negotiations for a reprovision scheme:

> We were under the impression that complete agreement on HR had been reached at the planning group, only to have the issue raised elsewhere. What happens is that officers report back to [the Councillor] and then have to shift their position. In fact he considers himself to be something of an expert. . . . In the end [he] has the mentally ill as a strong part of his platform, hence his leading interest.

Decentralization had implications for the organization of mental health services. The new neighbourhoods were seen to give particular opportunity for joint working with the DHA on resource centres and day centres which could offer support to mentally ill and elderly people confused in their own homes. These were to be the key services of the future, if resources to support them could be identified.

Such prospects engendered a high level of interest in reprovision from within the council during the early period of decision-making. There was the possibility that the council might take a central co-ordinating role in the future of mental health services. For a brief period, early in 1984, the LBI pursued a radical plan for decentralizing psychogeriatric services from Friern. Officers were instructed to come up with this plan by the chair of the social services sub-committee on mental health. In planning team discussion, while not agreeing with the DHA proposals for resettlement on the Whittington Hospital site (the Highgate wing, now known as Highgate Parkside), they had not previously put forward any alternative to them.

The plan suggested that a total of fifteen 'ordinary houses' could be adapted for the resettlement of the resident Friern psychogeriatric population. Each house would give seven or eight places in what would be a staffed group home. Three back-up centres would be provided in order to

'out-post' psychogeriatric day care and multidisciplinary expertise from the District General Hospitals so as to get it as near to the neighbourhood level as possible.

It was further argued that

provision needs to be made in the neighbourhood psychogeriatric units for NHS staff on round the clock duty but *not* on a living in basis.[9]

While the DHA was willing to fund a pilot scheme involving the use of LBI's homes for elderly people to provide for a small number of Friern patients, they could not support this degree of change. Their reasons were to become much clearer when the community health council made a further challenge to their proposals, which is discussed later.

Looking across the range of its plans, at the end of several years of negotiation with the LBI and voluntary organizations, the DHA could certainly have been considered to have made the giant leap which the RHA asked of it. Adjustment was made, albeit with senior officers constantly expressing misgivings about sacrificing the mentally ill on the altar of town hall politics. As the chair of the council's committee on mental health commented

Each side had to compromise. The local authority had to learn that the Health Authority wish to be involved in community care. It has happened through the Joint Consultative Committee.

There were essentially two phases of the adjustment. In the first, a range of non-NHS projects, many of them fortuitously in the offing prior to the Friern initiative, were accepted as provision for long-stay patients. Critics saw this as no more than the DHA sub-contracting the provision of staffed group homes. This type of provision, novel only in the sense that staff might live-in rather than visit to support clients, had historically in any case been provided outside the NHS. The sub-contracting allowed the Whittington site to be used for the minority of the long-stay population who were judged to require continuing NHS rehabilitation and the elderly with dementia, few of whom were thought capable of benefiting from community housing. The DHA did not move towards a centre of service in the neighbourhood offices of the LBI or in voluntary sector non-profit-making companies offering work to the ex-long-stay hospital resident.

A watershed followed in which, in a second phase of adjustment, the DHA set limits to its willingness to respond to the demands of other agencies. A year and a half after the LBI's proposals for neighbourhood nursing care had been rejected, the voluntary organizations supported the CHC in a further suit for an alternative to hospital provision for the psychogeriatric population within what was now the public plan for Friern of the health authority. Knowing that planning team pressure had failed, CHC members took the unusual step of formally objecting to the health authority proposals. For the CHC to exercise such a right of objection was not in itself uncommon, but for the objection to be laid to a significant *development* of service was so, since they might usually be expected to favour development. For the DHA it meant filibustering as the very lightest penalty when plans were already behind schedule because of the onset of the Griffiths reorganization. At the worst, the DHA might be forced by the Minister for Health to change its policy. The chair of the DHA, seemingly in some desperation, appealed to the CHC to reconsider exercising its right of objection. However, the appeal went ahead to be lodged with the minister.

For their part, DHA planners insisted that no more than half the psychogeriatric population at Friern could be resettled outside hospital conditions. The chair of the planning team, as a consultant psychiatrist, no doubt defended this cautious view in part because there was no psychogeriatrician in post to cover the Islington wards at Friern who might have been able to take responsibility for a more risky strategy. It was clear that she was not disturbed by the political issues involved. In attendance at the CHC meeting where the Friern plan was debated she argued

> The elderly are most badly done by [in terms of the extent of provision] in Friern. We hope the [LBI] group home pilot scheme will be a success and could be extended, we hope that at least forty out of the eighty on Highgate could therefore be catered for. Having said that a substantial number in Friern are suffering from physical ailments as well. It's obviously a matter of opinion about hospital places. Planning is a dynamic process for what we hope eventually is a comprehensive service. Community working gives us a chance to be more active, if you will, in a political sense.

The LBI had reluctantly accepted the DHA position, influenced by its sense that the Health Service was evidently genuinely interested in developing more community-oriented schemes. Council members felt that they would just get 'a lot of hot air' blown back at them if they were to push the issue again to the higher level of the RHA. The DHA had, moreover, agreed in principle to fund the placement of twenty-one patients in three LBI schemes centred on the council's homes for elderly people. One of these schemes was in fact the pilot group home for the elderly of the kind which the LBI had wished for the whole psychogeriatric population at Friern.

Following the CHC intervention, the minister held the documents for almost a year. Behind the scenes the DHSS had been making moves to get the parties to the dispute to agree on revisions to the DHA proposals. By this time (in 1986) a psychogeriatrician was at last in post to advise on planning proposals for the district and a 'core team' with a psychologist and a social worker had assessed many patients at Friern. The trend of the core team thinking was to move further away from hospital-like provision. Thus the dispute to some extent was settling itself. Finally the minister ruled that the DHA could provide up to fifty-five hospital beds for elderly people on the Highgate Parkside site, a figure which included 14 for short-stay assessment with long-stay beds.

In the middle of 1988 the DHA and the council were sufficiently in agreement to organize a joint conference on progress in mental health services. This was a confident and morale-boosting affair which put on show the achievement of the first phase of adjustment. Those attending from outside the borough were impressed with the level of achievement. In a crowded series of presentations, users' representatives spoke as well as those from the voluntary sector and statutory sector. The latter put particular emphasis on their efforts to try to move away from the 'enforced group living' of the group home model, to provide highly supported flats and to work on proposals for drop-in centres. This shift was favoured by users, one of whom argued that

> what is needed are teams of people – carers who can stay with some-one for a short time to help people adjust after hospital, or at the time of a crisis, or to give the family a break. These people [she continued] could be at a mental health centre or neighbourhood offices. Such schemes work in Derbyshire, why not in Islington?

The extent to which the DHA was making efforts to respond to the expressed needs of its consumers and to pressures from the social work and voluntary sector network should therefore not be under-emphasized. There was much more movement, under the stimulus of the Islington culture, than was being experienced in other districts. The DHA had even given a small grant to the users' organization, 'Islington Forum', originally assisted in its setting up by the Good Practices in Mental Health organization. Here they could claim justly to be in the forefront of change. The LBI's social services committee turned down the request from the Forum for funds, owing to its own overspending.

As Table 7 shows, however, these proposals for change did not make any significant impact on the schedule for reprovision already agreed. Mental health centres, which might have co-ordinated the domiciliary rescue service, were almost as far away as ever from implementation. There was a sense of there being 'too little too late' and representatives from the voluntary sector warned against 'the financial and managerial need to close a hospital [being] confused with community care'. A planning process which had been so strongly influenced by the availability of land and buildings, moving from Highgate Parkside outward, had still to evolve to fit the individual needs of clients: 'giving patients a choice between schemes could probably only be developed after they had left hospital'.

The deficiencies in planning to which the voluntary sector drew attention were to lead to the creation later in the year of a league of associations to press for joint planning and joint implementation between the statutory and non-statutory agencies. This initiative did not succeed. The DHA had by this stage suspended the large planning team on which non-NHS agencies were represented, on the grounds that implementation rather than planning was the main task facing officers, who would not be able to cope with both. This move effectively closed channels for further opposition to

Table 7 Islington: the changing disposition of Friern replacement beds

		1983	1985	1988
Acute		90 (60)[a]	90 (60)[a]	90 (60)[a] but proposed that 23 be designated for elderly people
Long-stay	NHS	160 (30)[a] in units of 30–50 places	30 (30)[a]	35 (30)[a]
Long-stay	non-NHS	To be phased in later	92	100
Psychogeriatric	NHS	10–20 assessment, 90 long-stay	14 80	18 50
Psychogeriatric	non-NHS	To be phased in later	14 LBI pt III[b]	21 LBI[b] 40 housing association

Notes: [a] Figures in parentheses are for general hospital beds in Islington already open in 1983.
[b] LBI = London Borough of Islington.

the DHA position and set a firm limit to the process of adjustment. From this point onward, strategy-making was conducted at a senior officers' forum internal to the DHA.

The health authority's resistance to pressure from voluntary organizations paved the way for a process of negotiated NHS withdrawal from close involvement with the LBI. The problems were essentially the same ones that accounted for the reluctance of the DHA to make large adjustments in the early stages. There was concern about an apolitical organization becoming involved in negotiations with a political one, councillors' committee decisions affecting the development of community services adversely, and about the non-viability of the LBI as a public organization. Its mortgaging strategy had not come off, since a Conservative government had been re-elected in 1987. Despite the small amounts of money involved, the council's mental health services were being subjected to the same percentage cuts as those applied to social services in general – about 10 per cent. As fast as Friern services were appearing, non-Friern clients were experiencing a service cut. The fear was that Friern resources would be used to bolster up the non-Friern, mainstream, LBI service.

Obviously there was no hope of any matching commitment from the LBI to the creation of services for people in the community. How far, in 1990, had the council fallen from the heady ambitions of its decentralization initiative. Politically the concern of members had shifted away from social services, which were no longer so fashionable. Devolution of the Inner London Education Authority's work to the borough councils had become a major municipal issue. For the time being mental health was off the agenda. This did not mean that no collaborative schemes were pursued. The DHA did agree to 'buy in' places for Friern patients at LBI day centres, as a temporary measure introduced because of delays experienced in the development of the permanent reprovision day activity projects. But it meant that there was no possibility of joining the LBI in its plan to turn the council homes for elderly people into neighbourhood resource centres offering a range of services. Although the schemes for transfer of elderly patients from Friern to two homes for the elderly were implemented successfully, this scheme was not to be replicated as the council had earlier hoped.

The argument advanced in this book of course considers the DHA to be just as subject to political intervention in its action as the council. A key element underplayed in the Friern programme was that the savings set aside for priority services development within Islington, of £0.5 million per annum, disappeared – sacrificed to the moral imperative of maintaining as much as possible of the district's acute general medicine capacity. As the district treasurer himself was to comment, underfunding of pay awards by central government had forced the district to 'mortgage' the savings on acute services retrenchment. This strategy could not unreasonably be compared to the council's strategy for borrowing money from City financiers.

Conclusion

Islington Health Authority began from a position of corporate strength, with key district management team members interested and involved in planning with support from a Left-leaning caucus of leading authority members. With consultant psychiatrists and nursing officers agreeable to the local authority and voluntary organizations playing a major role in re-provision, the DHA was able to substantially withdraw from sheltered provision for long-term mentally ill people. This solution took the national planning process much further from Banstead, and even Torbay, with a wide variety of types of permanent accommodation being planned. The radicalism of the position was more than clear from the comment of a Friern psychiatrist working for a neighbouring district that 'Islington has its own fantasies to work out'.

With a local authority that was keen to be engaged in the development process and with experienced voluntary organizations working in the borough, the DHA was able to move a long way from its initial caution. Nevertheless, it began from an assessment of what land and buildings were on offer. Its work did not stem from popular concerns or pressure, nor were proposals built around the choices of patients themselves. There was no Blue Horse of Cavallo to be paraded along Upper Street (the main thoroughfare of the borough). This is a significant lack because if an event of this kind were to happen anywhere within the Friern and Claybury catchment areas, then it would surely have happened within radical Islington. Two tenants' associations were involved by an enthusiastic neighbourhood officer for the social services department but this was one-off, weakly articulated instance of community participation in a project support group. What stands out instead is that developments were planned within a professional bargaining process.

While responding to public pressure, the DHA drew the line at formally decentralizing its planning process and ceding power within it. This was evident both at the time of suspension of the planning team and later in the decision not to agree to the multi-agency forum proposed by the voluntary organizations. There was also the need, financially, not to support the LBI too greatly, since every property purchase strengthened the council's profligate approach to service delivery. The DHA would be in danger of assisting the council *vis-à-vis* central authority while weakening its own position through the loss of part of its health domain. The DHA's position on mental health centres was somewhat quixotic. They were both keenly desired and searched for and yet not quite believed in, with not one single site for such a centre being firmly identified in the first five years of planning.

Waltham Forest: carrying out the reprovision order

In the early period the DHA accepted reprovision in principle but rejected it on the costing assumptions the RHA was making. This was plainly stated, and minuted, at the critical meeting of the RHA in July 1983 at which the chairmen of both Hampstead and Waltham Forest Health Authorities participated.

> It was the view of clinicians in Waltham Forest, supported by the DHA, that the closure of Claybury Hospital was not viable within the resources suggested. The RHA was asked not to make a decision in favour of closure against the advice of the medical profession, before the user districts were confident that it would be financially viable.[10]

Given that revenue was not going to increase significantly, the RHA would be in effect replacing a cheap hospital with cheap community services. That the RHA would be unlikely to change its position could presumably have been anticipated. Given the restrictions on growth in the health service across the country, and the enforced 'steady state' in London, this was a highly improbable scenario in North East Thames. It was probably rather surprising to regional officers that Waltham Forest maintained its view that a better-than-asylum service could not be provided within the financial limits which were being laid down.

The decision to oppose the RHA was one which drew on the views of both clinical and non-clinical staff in the districts. But the pressure which the RHA could bring to bear on the members and officers of the DHA in order to ensure the implementation of its policy was considerable. Within six months, the opposition of officers had collapsed. Compromise was reached by planning and management staff with their counterparts at the RHA by means of 'adjustments' to staff costs/mix. In other words cheaper, untrained or less well qualified staff would make up a larger proportion of the complement for the new units than the DHA had originally proposed. Clinical freedom gave the 'dissident' consultant psychiatrists more power, however, and they were not inclined to compromise. Their opposition caused the Waltham Forest DHA to pass a formal resolution requiring them to co-operate with reprovision in 1984. Despite this action, regional officers had to make a number of overtures to the consultants to try to win them round to supporting the reprovision policy. Their public opposition was to last, however, until the summer of 1985.

Although a settlement was made at an early stage between the two sides of planners and administrators at the RHA and DHA, a period of go-slow and implementation on the narrowest interpretation of the policy was to follow. The acute admission service for the district was based at Claybury rather than the DGH, and the local authority provided only one day centre in the borough. There was no history of attempts to develop a local service within Waltham Forest with the exception of the community mental health centre, opened by 'a few crazy people out there' (beyond Claybury), as one of its founders self-effacingly put it. Local participants in planning had not proved themselves enthusiastic about shifting the centre of services into the district, for all the lengthy deliberation of the joint care planning team within the Redbridge and Waltham Forest AHA. Claybury closure was therefore seen as a policy owned by regional officers rather than people within the DHA or the Claybury unit management team.

The anxiety of the RHA's officers to achieve local ownership can be all the better appreciated in these circumstances. Neither local authority nor health authority members were in touch with reprovision. On the 'Health' side this was because the DHA was very much chief-officer led. The chief officer, the district general manager, had entrusted reprovision to the mental health unit. District officers had other work to do associated with the reorganization of acute services. The DGM maintained, even in 1988, that unless the RHA kept a firm hand on reprovision, it might easily find the initiative unsupported at the local level.

Why was it locally unsupported?

Much can be explained by the lack of pressure on the DHA from community representatives in the CHC, from voluntary organizations and from the borough council. Waltham Forest was a completely different environment for decision-making from that of Islington. The council did not have the municipal ambitions of its inner-city Labour-controlled neighbours, being 'hung' (under no overall political control) from 1982 to 1986. Officers took the opportunity to avoid politicization of issues where possible. While members supported the CHC's wish to see a council-co-ordinated Health Liaison Committee set up for the borough, officers warned them that

> as the Council's policy toward health service resource allocation is one of clear opposition to the Government's, and to Waltham Forest Health Authority's acceptance of them, improvements to consultative machinery is unlikely to achieve the impact [on health policy] we seek.

The more formal the type of committee adopted, the greater such probably deleterious impact would be, since

> at Officer level, it would be likely that the Health Authority's officers would become increasingly cautious in their discussions with the Council's officers to lessen the chance of intelligence being gathered to inform criticism of the Health Authority's policies and decisions. This would frustrate much that is currently being achieved.[11]

Women's issues and disability issues did come to the fore after the Labour group took control in 1986, but in a period where local government nationally was already retrenching, the impact of these new concerns was diluted.

An additional reason for inactivity in this policy area was the lack of interest of the outgoing Redbridge and Waltham Forest AHA in a funded priority services growth strategy. As already noted, the RHA was not confident that this AHA would have been capable of solving the mental hospital problem.

The decision-making process was strongly influenced by the fact that reprovision was being managed from within Claybury. Unit officers worked in the main hospital building while the offices of the district management team were located in a fine period building close by, in which the health authority held its meetings. In Islington and Haringey planners and administrators with a mental health brief worked from offices within the district general hospital complexes. They were thus not subject to the danger of even a sentimental attachment to the architectural and landscaping attractions of the mental hospital estates. Nor did they necessarily feel the sense of obligation to residents and staff at the asylums which would be inherent in the neighbouring relationship that existed within Waltham Forest DHA. Finally, loyalty to the traditional nursing mode of care would tend to be considerably stronger in a setting where that loyalty had to be demonstrated every day.

The approach to reprovision taken by mental health managers was that it amounted to a geographical dispersal of Claybury services. The new service would be achieved by the purchase of sites and buildings for nursing homes with attached day centres. This disposition is outlined in Table 8. The scope for providing 'new' types of service such as dispersed single-person housing with peripatetic staff support, or for work co-operatives, was thought to be very limited. The reprovided nursing service would have a focus at a new upgraded 'core' unit, with 130 beds for short-stay admissions. This would be located somewhere centrally within the borough. In theory it might have been proposed at Claybury had the same handiness to the borough applied as at Friern for western Haringey. But the hospital was not in the borough and in any case was inaccessible. Only two bus routes reached it and there was no convenient London Underground or British Rail station.

This picture emerging of a disaggregated localized Claybury was likened to a 'jumbo jet that has crashed and broken into small pieces' by one mental health worker. But the plan could be interpreted, in one sense, as strikingly more ambitious than that of Islington's first efforts. Planning officers aimed to move mental health away from general medicine by building an acute unit for short-stay admissions on a cleared site within a residential area. Unit planners also argued that the nursing home and hostel provision should *not* be placed on the redundant hospital land, which was becoming available as centralization of general acute services on the DGH proceeded. Nevertheless, as part of the compromise with the RHA, they agreed that such a plan was impractical because of the shortage of land and suitable large houses in the borough.

In the absence of a framework of adjustment to the work of other agencies, the clinical and vocational sense of client group ownership remained strong. Clearly the need to consider redeployment of Claybury staff, and

Table 8 Waltham Forest: the changing disposition of Claybury replacement beds

		1983	1985	1988
Acute		116 (12)[a]	90–110 (12)[a]	110 (12)[a]
Long-stay	NHS	134[b] in nursing homes 65 in staffed hostels	120 5 units each of 24 places	96 4 units of 24
Long-stay	non-NHS	12	12	14
Psychogeriatric	NHS	One assessment ward, the rest of provision to be made up as half of long-stay places above	Assessment 45 long-stay	Assessment 48 2 × 24-place nursing homes
Psychogeriatric	non-NHS	None	35 in LBWF home[c]	50 2 LBWF homes[c]

Notes: [a] Figures in parentheses are for general hospital beds in Waltham Forest already open in 1983.

   [b] Feasibility study allowed for the possibility that some nursing home provision could be run by non-NHS agencies.

   [c] LBWF = London Borough of Waltham Forest.

for Waltham Forest as managing district to take the lead in such redeployment, meant that the model of the future service would have to provide a substantial body of work for nurses. Demobilization to non-NHS agencies was not a favoured option. The Waltham Forest DHA could be considered more autarchic in other policy areas, responding to public pressure in promoting 'Well Woman' clinics for example. But in mental health development and Claybury reprovision, it was clearly controlled by the centre. The proposal to develop the acute unit in a residential area was an exceptional guided action, planned on nursing and medical advice within the unit.

Whereas Islington shifted considerably from its earlier plan for hospital to hospital reprovision to involve other agencies, such adjustment was not planned by the mental health unit in Waltham Forest. Unit officers did make contact with two local housing associations. At length, one of them was invited to submit proposals for new-build sheltered housing on a corner of a hospital site. Generally though, in the early years, it was felt that since the associations offered no more than housing management there was little to be gained by striking deals for the delivery of care. Apart from the provision of twenty places by the association invited in, and twelve places which were to be provided by the local branch of MIND, provision for the long-stay population was to be developed and managed by the DHA.

In some respects this plan for reprovision was idiosyncratic. A local agency, known as Outward Housing, with which a member of the DHA was heavily involved, had for some years been setting up schemes to take local people out of the district mental handicap hospital, Leytonstone House. But she was not approached for guidance on resettlement from Claybury. It was not thought that the council offered much to the reprovision programme. Council officers appeared to concur with the view of the DHA that the dependency of the patients made it primarily an NHS medical and nursing issue.

Interestingly the council did not initially see itself as having a role in reprovision. This is in complete contrast to Islington. Partly this stemmed from the fact that much time and effort had been put into work on mental handicap initiatives, through which a lot of innovative projects for deinstitutionalization had been set up. Partly it was to do with the fact that the DHA's mental health unit officers considered that there was little scope for non-nursing models of care for community schemes. Nevertheless, the local authority was naturally seen as a provider of sites for development in a borough where such sites were at a premium. Fortunately for the DHA it was not taking up a negotiating position requiring the NHS to fund, through reprovision moneys, substantial developments of council service before any sites or buildings might be made available. Social services officers were rather directing their efforts toward

> developing a strategy for achieving a community based mental health programme *complementary* to provision by the Health Service and voluntary sector. (my emphasis)

Accordingly council members were informed that

> The Claybury reprovision does not entail a major transfer of resources to the authority nor to the voluntary sector.[12]

In 1985 the local authority did agree proposals with the DHA to provide two twenty-five-place nursing homes for elderly people. Council officers were very keen to make this kind of provision because of a large shortfall in their directly managed provision for elderly people in general. It was clear that to an extent the fifty places would fill a gap in the building programme to which the local authority had committed itself but for which it was unable to find resources. Indeed, members felt this an unsatisfactory way of dealing with their own lack of funding when the issue came before the social services committee. The provision of the two homes for the resettlement of Claybury residents was to be the limit of the council's involvement. Later, social services officers were to regret their lack of drive to participate more in reprovision.

The non-statutory sector was almost conspicuous by its absence in this district. Again the reasons for this were complex. MIND had no history of service provision and had a thin membership in the borough. It was completely absorbed with the development of what was known as the 'Forest Community Project', after its inclusion for funding within the DHSS national *Care in the Community* pilot programme in 1983. On the other hand such organizations as the Mental After Care Association and the PRA were established in neighbouring boroughs, while East London and Springboard Housing Associations were heavily involved in resettlement of residents from the nearby Goodmayes Hospital. There was thus no obvious reason why this sector was not involved.

Waltham Forest DHA did have the most difficult task in terms of sheer labour, that is to manage the rundown of the hospital as provider of services, and to create a local service within the boundaries of its own district as a 'purchaser'. Moreover it was the largest single user of beds in the hospital, having more than 300 to transfer. Hampstead, faced with the same dual task at Friern, had only half as many patients to relocate within its own district boundary.

There were various accidents of history which contributed to the Waltham Forest cautious interpretation of reprovision as essentially a transfer of medical and nursing care. The literalness of this reprovision had both advantages and disadvantages. The director of nursing at Claybury was a key role-player in its planning, especially given the absence of consultant psychiatrists. Being 'totally committed to the process of closure', he felt that it presented an opportunity for the hospital to turn itself from an inward-looking to an outward-looking institution:

> If the rigid demarcation of staff's roles can be broken down we will get a much better service than at present. As far as the money goes, we will be saving a phenomenal amount on the upkeep of Claybury when the wards shut down and we will not have to fund the rigid shift system of the hospital in the new units. What we should see there is Charge Nurses with total control of the management of team shifts, the budget and the unit overall, thus a completely different system.[13]

Pejoratively, reprovision could be construed as a repotting of Claybury. But literal reprovision could also be seen as essential to 'ring-fence' resources around the chronic and elderly population who were most vulnerable to neglect. There was a lesser fear of dilution of resources than in Islington but this fear was still important, at least for the director of nursing:

My big concern is about rate-capping, and the possible effect that could have on Social Services provision of care on our behalf. . . . In my view the initial reprovision should be NHS led, managed and provided.[14]

The director's concerns may well have been allayed in the process of debate with the local authority representatives. But because of the apparent lack of interest of the social services department, at least where the long-stay population was concerned, DHA officers were not apprised of the potential ways in which council services might offer scope for development of reprovision initiatives.

The most important issue in the early stages of the planning process was about revenue funding. Here the consultant psychiatrists focused on two major concerns. The first was that the break-up of Claybury meant the break-up of specialist services such as psychotherapy which would be too expensive for each district to support. Second, by 1986 there was evidence that the 'easy', less dependent patients were being taken out of the hospital first and that the more disabled groups were being left behind. This would inevitably mean that the later stages of reprovision, implemented carefully, would mean more staff and more expense than was anticipated. It was suggested that sheltered facilities shared between districts should be provided, possibly on the Claybury site, for those who would continue to need asylum and could not be placed in the community. The consultants were in an isolated and less secure position than at Friern. Most of them did not have a base in the user district catchment areas from which they admitted patients (such as the respective DGHs) and so their own future was in jeopardy. They were also funded and employed directly by the RHA, rather than Waltham Forest DHA, since the latter was not, unlike Hampstead, a teaching district. Cynics suggested that they were only looking after their own interests in putting forward the proposals for multi district services on the Claybury site. Having failed to make these proposals during the feasibility studies and to develop a counter-strategy at that time, they were now, belatedly, after two years of non-co-operation, embarking on such a course of action, and attempting to discount the DHA's planning for Claybury reprovision of the intervening period.

The chairman and general manager of the regional health authority, both new appointments since NETRHA's 1983 closures decision, were 'determined to meet the consultants as allies'. At the local level managers were worried about the possibility of a further period of non-participation if the consultants did not get their way on the new proposals. They held a more sanguine view of the situation:

Region would tell them what to do. They're sick of them. They didn't break their hearts about non-cooperation last time.

After becoming formally reacquainted with the planning process, a group of the consultant psychiatrists produced their own critical review of district proposals. Diagnosing a number of what were termed 'structural' difficulties with the planning process they pointed out that:

> The hallmark of the 1982 proposals was of top-down planning, that is plans were formulated and presented at the administration level which disregarded the expertise of the clinical staff and resulted in them being alienated from the planning process.[15]

What was needed now was a new approach which allowed 'bottom-up planning':

> the clinical staff who actually have the experience and expertise with the patients they manage being involved in detailed operational planning.[16]

In discussion of elements of the 'user' district's plans, the intention of West Essex Health Authority to provide short-stay beds on the district's main general hospital site at the 'new town' of Harlow, was singled out for particular criticism. The move would amount to 'the total negation of the concept of community care'.[17] This was because patients from the Claybury catchment area of the district – Epping Forest – were held to regard themselves as Londoners who would be forced to travel to a town further away from their homes than Claybury. The consultants concluded their review by stating that

> At the present time there is no co-ordinated plan regarding future developments on Claybury reprovision.[18]

As part of a counter-proposal, it was argued that a kind of super-district be created for mental health services purposes, that would consist of the Epping Forest district in West Essex (population 100,000) and the borough of Waltham Forest. By means of this proposal the residents of Epping Forest would not have to travel to Harlow for treatment since the new catchment area would be provided with mental health services by a 'purpose built unit on the southern part of the Claybury site'.[19] The unit would also provide for a complex of sheltered accommodation designed for the rehabilitation of the most dependent patients in the hospital and for 'existing valued services' to be reprovided. Examples of such services were 'the nursing school, the postgraduate medical education facility, the library, the psychotherapy unit, the rehabilitation unit and the intensive care unit'.[20]

Thus, at the eleventh hour, there was a return to the ambitions of the old JCPT, which had based its assumptions on a similarly large scale 200 bed unit at Wanstead Hospital being available to serve Waltham Forest.

In the mean time, the officers of the Claybury management team, meeting with social services colleagues under the chairmanship of the district medical officer, had found a site for their own much smaller core unit for acute admissions from Waltham Forest. This was a sports-ground site which the council intended to sell. However, around the time of the 1986 elections to the council, the plans for this unit became entangled in a web of political difficulties. The consultant psychiatrists, given their counter-proposal, were hardly likely to be enthusiastic. Indeed, they argued that the site was too small to give the space necessary for an asylum. Then local residents, informed of the proposed development through the council's Town Planning Department, became greatly alarmed at the prospect of becoming neighbours to this unit. At a public meeting attended by more than 300 residents of the borough, which in itself indicated that mental health had, however briefly, become a local election issue, council members lost no opportunity to curry favour with the public.

Social services officers later confided to their DHA colleagues that they had been greatly embarrassed by members' behaviour. Ironically it was a member of the DHA, who had opposed closure in 1983 and was a ward councillor, who joined battle on the side of the disquieted public with some gusto. Since he happened to be chairman of the planning committee when the application was heard, he was in a position of some power at this juncture, where decisions about the reprovision of Claybury were concerned. Joining other councillors in expressing disappointment with the DHA's speakers at the public meeting, he argued that

> The DHA has failed dismally in planning to bring mental health patients out into the community. The public meeting was such a dismal failure on their behalf, without any professional speakers on their behalf present – and yet they had two years to do that. I'm a member of the DHA and I'm sickened by the way they've done that.

The planning application was turned down by the Committee, at a meeting which drew a sizeable audience. The DHA decided to withdraw to reconsider its position. It was one of those typical instances where mental health only became a public issue because of the threat to the community perceived by plans to place a large unit in the middle of a residential district.

Despite this reversal, unit planners and managers were not prepared to entertain the suggestions of Consultants on multi district admissions facilities for an enlarged catchment area that would have included Epping Forest as well as Waltham Forest. This was despite the fact that the siting of such facilities on hospital land would provide a means of overcoming the opposition of the general public. The Medical Committee had to compromise, since the DHA was determined to resubmit its planning application on the sports-ground site after undertaking further public consultation. After some dispute, the psychiatrists accepted the lesser attractions of a facility for Waltham Forest only, probably because six of them hoped to be employed from that base in the reprovided service. After negotiation with the RHA, it was agreed that the lesser total of 110 acute admission beds would be provided from the sports-ground site.

The general opposition attracted in this phase of reprovision could be partly attributed to the fact that the DHA had developed most of its plans through a small sub group of the wider Planning Team, which rarely met. Professionals from a number of disciplines felt excluded from the process. In 1987, following the débâcle over the sports-ground and the Consultant Psychiatrists publication of a counter plan, officers of the District Management Team, turned their full attention to mental health issues, for perhaps the first time since 1983. They became concerned that their lower level colleagues in the mental health unit had adopted a too literal nursing-focused reprovision strategy. Partly this concern had arisen because of the apparent difficulties in planning for Claybury staff to be given specific roles in the new services offered by reprovision. But it also partly arose from the particular epidemiological concerns of a new Director of Nursing at the DHA level. In his view the mental health unit plan did not give sufficient consideration to the needs of people with chronic illness who were not in Claybury, i.e. residents of Waltham Forest, many of whom had been discharged in previous years.

This pressure prompted a change in the unit approach and an attempt to widen the net of contributors to planning. The questions were so fundamental that the 'think-tank' officers' group within the planning team felt it would have to involve more people. As the unit general manager (UGM) commented:

> Initially, when I came over here it was just reprovision not development, and Claybury decided to do it as part of the unit team. . . . What we need, because we've got to draw up a comprehensive plan for the district is [that] we've got to look at how Community Mental Health Centres (CMHCs) work.

And as the chair of the group put it

> We do need to discuss CMHCs as an absolute idea, do we want them and where do we want them?

This was proof indeed that the hospital closure was treated as an imposition by the centre (in this case the RHA) and not as a task providing opportunities for the district. The RHA was asking for a simple transfer of care from Claybury to Waltham Forest to take place, and the mental health unit of the DHA was obliged to implement it. One member of the unit management team was quite clear that

> Waltham Forest had got its own plans for a community based service prior to the region's coming in and in all honesty could have done without the region stepping in – particularly in regard to the eventual decision of the Claybury consultants that they would not take part in the exercise. Region was more interested in talking about money

than the clinical problem. Also there was a problem that the region was being prescriptive.

Prompted by statutory obligations to consult the public on closures, the RHA in 1987 asked all districts to go through a public consultation process on their plans. Some, such as Haringey, Hampstead and Islington, where the local authorities were very active in this policy area, had already done so. Waltham Forest had not. Scrutinizing the document which unit officers produced, regional officers were unhappy with both the revenue costs attached to it, and what they considered to be its 'institutional feel'. The DHA was asked to reduce the number of acute beds proposed for the sports-ground, to involve housing associations in the provision of the nursing units for the long-stay population, and to disperse these units by creating smaller establishments.

These interventions provoked a spirited defence of the Waltham Forest intentions from Claybury headquarters, though some members of the wider planning team now established were less entrenched in their defence. They knew they would again have to compromise on revenue costs, since there had been a certain element of 'bidding up' in the submission to the RHA. For example the costings had included an inter-district school of nursing whereas the RHA argued that it would fund only the Waltham Forest element within such a school as part of the Waltham Forest plan. It would be up to the other districts to determine their own contribution from their reprovision resources to support such a school.

With regard to consideration of housing associations, unit officers had in any case substantially changed from their original nursing home position. The residental units to be built for the purpose were to be quite varied in design, and to be sub-divided into 'family' houses. One of the units was to be managed by a housing association and would allow for independent but supported living, in interconnected 'bedsit' apartments. The planning team also began to consider whether the consortium of agencies, which was involved in managing units for mentally handicapped people in the borough, could take over responsibility for some of the other residential units, with nursing care remaining the responsibility of the DHA.

Perhaps the most surprising development of this period (between 1988 and 1989) was the decision by *district* officers that the acute admissions unit planned for the sports-ground be sited instead on the DGH site, at Whipps Cross Hospital. Considering how much effort Claybury planners and managers had put into finding the site and fighting for it through the council's planning committee, this was both a surprising and an infuriating intervention.

In 1983 it had been thought by regional architects that the 110 acute psychiatric beds for reprovision could not be fitted in to the redevelopment of the whole Whipps Cross site planned at that stage, for lack of space. However, when senior officers in the district became concerned about the potential for a mini-asylum to rise up on the sports-ground, they investigated whether a smaller unit might be feasible at the DGH. Estates officers from the RHA and the DHA concurred that there was, just, enough room for a reduced number of eighty-five psychiatric department beds. This judgement allowed the DGM to push through the abandonment of the sports-ground proposal.

The determination of the district management board to carry through this change to the unit plan provoked a public conflict within the DHA. One of its ironies was that the psychiatrists were now falling into line behind their planners and managers in the mental health unit in order to defend the sports-ground 'core unit'. They had hitherto, of course, argued strongly that this site was too small for a busy, short stay, acute admissions facility. But faced with the loss of the opportunity for at least some kind of free standing mental health campus, that the threat of having to work from the Whipps Cross DGH site entailed, they were only too keen to join the argument with the District Management Board. The scene was now set for a confrontation between the mental health unit on the one side and the management executive of the DHA on the other.

This confrontation was brought out into the open in December 1988 at an ordinary meeting of the Waltham Forest Health Authority. Using the good offices of the Chairman of the District Medical Committee, who was a member of the Authority, a representative of the Claybury psychiatrists asked if he might address the meeting on the subject of the acute admissions unit. Such an address was highly irregular, and at first the Chairman of the Authority asked for time to consider it, while the debate among his members began. His reluctance was no doubt also influenced by his knowledge that the psychiatrist's contribution could well resurrect old conflicts over the closure of Claybury itself. Nevertheless, he did agree to the Authority hearing the psychiatrist's speaker, who began by stating that:

> What we're saying is not only the view of the Psychiatric Division but of the Mental Health Planning Team which has been working hard for the last five years. The view is unanimous from those of them delivering the service that they'd be extremely unhappy if the unit was at Whipps.
>
> When considering where to place the unit we had two things in mind. Firstly enough space – under the roof and outside and not reproducing institutional practices. Secondly the people we look after are often extremely disturbed. They do need an amount of privacy.
> . . .
>
> 80–90 per cent of patients do not need heavy psychiatric technology and because of that we've got the [sports-ground] site. The district agreed that for the last two years and we've been increasing in enthusiasm that it will provide a good service for Waltham Forest.

When responding, the DGM could not but refer to the fact that the psychiatric division (of the District Medical Committee) had been arguing for a very different service for much of the early period of planning:

> There's been two years' enthusiasm from psychiatrists. Until last year a body of psychiatrists was planning for a Waltham Forest and West Essex service on the Claybury site.

In the debate of the health authority, it was noteworthy that the two representatives of the medical profession in the district who were members, did not support the psychiatrist's position. Only one of the other non-medical members felt strongly against the Whipps Cross plan. The authority remained loyal to the DGM. The proposal for the DGH beds was voted easily through. The mental health unit general manager, who had been involved in reprovision from the outset, sat silently through the DGM's presentation of the new proposal with which her officers disagreed. Here were unusual scenes indeed for those steeped in local public administration. The unit was being demoted. Some expected that unit officers would resign, but they were proved wrong.

Yet the acute admission unit was not the most controversial issue in reprovision. This was undoubtedly the MIND *Care in the Community* project. Since it had been conceived as part of the DHSS pilot programme for community care in England, it had an independent status from Claybury and Friern closure. The project was, however, set up in order to resettle long-stay patients from Claybury in the community. The DHA and local authority were thus due to 'pick up' its funding (probably from joint finance) after the trial three-year period of central government funding. Within what it entitled the 'Forest Community Project', MIND hoped to resettle at least twelve and up to eighteen patients in four houses in different parts of the borough.

From the beginning the Claybury unit management team didn't entirely have faith in this project. The proposition which MIND made was that chronic patients could be supported in the community without full-time residential staffing. The unit view was that a fundamental error of judgement was involved in this proposition. Officers were agreed that it was possible to withdraw some support from patients once they had settled in community settings, but in their view such withdrawal could be done only gradually. At the outset twenty-four-hour on-site support would have to be given for patients who were resettled in the houses. There were many other issues about methods of care for patients leaving Claybury which aroused heated controversy, with health service officers feeling that there was a lack of sufficient consistent input in the houses. By the middle of 1988 tensions between MIND and the DHA were running high. One patient had been readmitted to hospital after a period in which he had not been eating properly and had lost a considerable amount of weight.

The front-line workers, for their part, were exhausted after bearing the brunt of the rejection of community care as a concept by some key Claybury staff. Local authority officers party to the development of the pilot project were uncomfortable go-betweens, with the assistant director of the social services department, making efforts to try to bring about a resolution of the conflict.

There were underlying personality clashes of an unusually bitter nature, and the saga of conflict was clearly damaging to the morale of the project organizers. In 1989 all of its staff were looking for other jobs. Of the three original leaders, one had retired because of sickness and the other two had left. The saddest part of the affair was that though there were successive DHA and local authority inquiries into the running of the project, the care given was generally considered to be reasonably good. It seemed to many that the project was a victim of a diffuse process of kickback from the asylum. As the Kings Fund, one of four investigators, concluded:

> From the outset the Project was viewed as a competitor to the services provided at Claybury Hospital. Managers did not expect the Project to gain funding and had no confidence that an 'inexperienced' organisation could run such a service. On the Project side, there was an assumption that 'the hospital is wrong and we have the right answers'.
>
> It is to be anticipated that residents moving from a long stay hospital into the community will encounter crises from time to time. . . . However there do not appear to be jointly agreed arrangements for dealing with such crises. . . . As a result placements are seen to have 'broken down' and residents have returned to Claybury Hospital amid recriminations.[21]

Conclusion

In Waltham Forest a number of factors contributed to the DHA behaving as a controlled type of authority. There were three major 'absences' which went some way to account for this. First, there was the absence of pressure from the social services and housing departments of the council, either for a particular form of service to be planned or for the DHA to contract with the local authority for reprovision projects. This was all the more surprising and problematic given that the social services department was itself very much under-provided in its facilities for the long-term support of mentally ill people.

Second, there was the absence of voluntary organizations and the CHC in the planning process. In later years MIND and the CHC did send representatives to the wider planning team, but they had not taken part in the development work of the sub-group chaired by the District Medical Officer. This meant that the level of knowledge about and interest in reprovision remained low among the informed public. There would be little chance of any community views coming to the fore if the CHC and voluntary sector played a weak role.

Third, there was the absence of officers of the district management team, aside from the DMO, whose position was rather more peripheral after the Griffiths reorganization. Whereas in the Islington district the team was heavily involved and saw the reprovision initiative as an opportunity for the wider district priority services strategy to be taken forward, in Waltham Forest the DMT handed the task down to the unit. The task was thus interpreted narrowly as one of reproviding Claybury facilities, rather than widely to favour other local organizational interests.

The RHA was seen to have smashed local potential for developing community care in its reprovision initiative and to have thwarted would-be product champions. It was difficult for regional officers even to stimulate a guided mode of reprovision in which they could support local product champions developing models of service distinctive of Waltham Forest, for instance by an expansion of the community mental health centre established so early on in Leytonstone and apparently giving such good opportunity for innovation.

Aside from the pressures on unit managers arising from their location at Claybury, the stance of the consultant psychiatrists during the critical planning years meant that reprovision proposals would have to be reasonably cautious if some degree of harmony between planners, nurse managers and clinicians was to be preserved. Implanted into this framework, the MIND project pointed up the key issue of competitiveness between nursing and social care and played a part in arousing the interests of district officers who had hitherto been happy to delegate reprovision to their mental health unit colleagues.

Haringey: the case of the would-be guided authority

The arrangement of health services to serve the people of Haringey was such that the district health authority had the appearance of an organizational oddment or remainder. The population resident in the western part of the borough was served by the Islington district general hospital, the Whittington. Haringey's main general hospital site, the North Middlesex (NMH), serving the eastern part of the borough, Tottenham, was actually situated just outside the borough boundary in Enfield. While being the Haringey DGH it also covered the catchment area of Edmonton, forming the south-eastern part of the Enfield borough. A subsidiary site for the DGH, St Ann's, in which some acute admissions for mental illness were accepted, was situated within the borough boundary in south Tottenham. However, this hospital was being rundown as a centre for acute general medicine in line with centralization on the main district site in Enfield (see Figure 2, p. 48).

This complex arrangement meant that there was no obvious central location at which a new district-based mental health service could be developed. As in Waltham Forest there had been little attempt to build up such a service prior to the initiative of the NETRHA. There had historically been vague proposals to develop a whole district service centred on acute psychiatry at St Ann's. How realistic these proposals were was open to question. It was the district administrator's view that a service local to Haringey would not have emerged without the regional initiative on Friern and Claybury.

It had proved enormously difficult to get resources for the far lesser task of upgrading the two wards dedicated to psychiatry at St Ann's. These wards and the day hospital managed by the district had previously been accommodated at the North Middlesex. In 1980 an AHA members' monitoring group visited the NMH wards and produced a confidential report which contained stinging criticisms. Members urged that the planned move of these treatment facilities to upgraded accommodation at St Ann's Hospital be carried out as soon as possible. It was clear that some of the problems were to do with a lack of management input to mental health. Indeed the consultant psychiatrist involved in the issue wanted the authority to undertake an independent inquiry into that management.

Members of the district management team of 1981/2 did not appear to enjoy great respect from their colleagues. In the eyes of one close observer within the public service they were 'low calibre staff' to whom 'the word strategy was foreign'. They were 'putty to the winds of political opportunism'.

According to a member of the new team which succeeded those staff, Haringey had a reputation as 'the armpit of the region'. Judged on the basis of these impressions, Haringey certainly started out as a second-grade district.

Not only did the DHA start with these disadvantages but also it had the task of reproviding for patients both at Friern and Claybury. In effect officers had to organize twice as much planning input in maintaining a decision-making presence in the bodies co-ordinating the closures. Haringey, as the DMO pointed out, thus had

> the unique distinction of being the only District to be served by both affected hospitals. Thus the Region's separation of activities [in the feasibility studies], logical from their viewpoint, left us with considerable difficulties, conceptual, logistic and financial.[22]

A total of nearly 450 places in the community would have to be provided if all Haringey's allotted hospital residents were to move back to the district (see Table 9). This number was half as much again as any of the other districts would need to plan for. Would the DHA possibly be able to achieve this scale of planning?

A very large ethnic minority population was resident in the borough, which in fact constituted a majority population in some electoral wards.

Table 9 Haringey: the changing disposition of Friern and Claybury replacement beds

		1983[a]	1985[b]	1988[b]
Acute		94 (52)[c]	150 (52)[c]	140 (47)[c]
Long-stay	NHS	75 per cent of beds to be in hospital-like accommodation to include 63 beds at St Ann's Hospital	90 in three 30-place units	111
Long-stay	non-NHS	25 per cent to be in supported accommodation with day care rehab.	136	102
Psychogeriatric	NHS	Range of hospital and NHS nursing home provision	71 with 18–24 for assessment	70 (22)[cd]
Psychogeriatric	non-NHS	None	56 8 × 10-place homes	27

Notes: [a] Planning for London Borough of Haringey (LBH) area.
   [b] Planning for LBH area plus extra-territorial Edmonton.
   [c] Figures in parentheses are for general hospital beds in Haringey already open.
   [d] New ward opened at St Ann's during reprovision period.

Planners therefore faced sensitive issues about treatment of black patients. Particularly prominent was the excessively high rate of compulsory admissions from the Afro-Caribbean communities in comparison with levels of such admissions among people classified as 'White European'. Despite the salience of these issues, it took many years for any proposals to be advanced which were aimed at addressing some of the evident inequalities of treatment and care.

   The alignment of western Haringey with the health services of the Islington Health Authority, and of the eastern half of the district with Enfield to the north, meant that the future of the Haringey DHA as an organization was in jeopardy all the way through the Claybury and Friern process. In 1988 a proposal for a merger with the Hampstead district almost came to fruition. In 1990, under the terms of the Prime Minister's reform of the NHS, the chairman and the district general manager proposed that the North Middlesex Hospital become an independent trust. The 'unviability' of the DHA was reflected in the political factionalism and acrimony of its meetings. In no sense was there a corporate strength of the kind which was enjoyed in Islington. As in Waltham Forest, issues at the level of the authority members were dominated by the rationalization of general medicine, and particularly the issue of the two-sited DGH.

Relations between the members of the local council, the London Borough of Haringey (LBH) and the members of the health authority were always extremely difficult. Up to 1987 joint planning had been almost entirely restricted to matters of joint finance. There were old political scores to settle relating back to AHA days. The AHA had been 'politically hung to the point that the Enfield Conservative element cancelled out the Haringey Labour element' and where consequently 'stalemate existed' on many issues.[23] The chairman of the new Haringey DHA had been a local Conservative politician. He was generally considered to be politically fair in his handling of DHA business, and was willing to accede to the appointment of a former Labour leader of the council to a senior management post within the health authority. But naturally he also held his own personal, but influential, views on important issues such as municipal provision of services. Haringey Council was controlled by the Labour party throughout the 1980s: its representatives on the DHA were implacably and consistently opposed to the rationalization proposals. Between one group of members on the authority who invariably followed the chairman's leadership, and the Labour group who opposed them, were 'floaters' in the middle. Officers could not depend with any certainty up to the time of the authority meetings that their arguments on any one issue would be supported.

It was particularly hard for the DHA to envisage joint planning with the voluntary sector since that meant liaison with the council, as the agency grant-aiding most of the established organizations. In Islington the corporate 'soft Left' culture amongst members of the DHA meant that officers were more open to adjust to local authority initiatives. In Haringey there was no such culture to draw on. In addition mental health did not enjoy the high profile which it achieved within the council committee structure in Islington. Bromley's work suggests that members did not have a concern with the development of any favoured form of service in the wake of closure:

we need to recall that important as the closure of the two Hospitals will be, in no sense do these matters form any central consideration for Haringey Members. The Chair and some four or five Members of the Social Services Committee are closely informed and highly knowledgeable but they, understandably, are in a distinct minority. In so far as there has been a concern, by Members as a whole, it has been more, again understandably, about the prospect of job losses at Friern rather than the fate of individual patients.[24]

The upshot of this was that DHA officers concerned with the implementation of reprovision did enjoy a lot of action space to work out proposals for new services. This was not the situation of adjustment that existed in Islington but it did allow a debate between fieldworkers to flourish.

The beginnings of mental health strategy development in Haringey, during the RHA-co-ordinated feasibility studies, were marked by an entrenched conflict on the issue of whether closure on *any* terms was feasible.

> These meetings were sometimes allowed to generate into wrangles in which three of the four psychiatrists would take the line that the exercise was both impractical (financially) and professionally undesirable. The three psychiatrists did not withdraw physically but in terms of a proper contribution to constructing a costed plan, their contribution was negligible.[25]

It was impossible for administrative and planning staff to follow their advice in any submission to the RHA – since they had been asked to consider what services would be required if the hospitals were to close.

That this line should be taken was a surprise to regional officers. On 4 May 1983 one of their number involved in planning reprovision wrote to the RMO and RNO to say that at the meeting of the Haringey Feasibility Group which she had attended the previous day,

> The discussion was to be based on a perfectly reasonable draft document drawn up by the Social Services man. After 2¼ hours we had reached page six, baffled at every turn by Dr A, who monopolised the discussion, reiterating his views that Friern should not only remain but be expanded! Dr B was less intensive but equally committed to regarding the Group as the forum for arguing for the status quo.
>
> I – and to be fair, the Haringey people – tried to make clear that the . . . Group's function is to plan a comprehensive district service for Haringey and that there were other forums to discuss Friern's role.
>
> I tried to hint that the Regional Team of Officers would be unwilling to spend an afternoon on 10 May, hearing once again the arguments of the Friern Consultants. Your object in coming was to help firm up the Group's proposals.
>
> I fear however that if Dr A is there he will again be obstructive. He is one of the Friern role-players.

This was an inauspicious beginning on two counts. First, because implementation would be extremely difficult if the local plan was not owned by the key care professions who would be responsible for resettling the patients. Second, because it meant that the planners who had to write up proposals at the regional behest would have to be very cautious and just adapt 'safe' models of district services from consultations with the experts in other places. This they did. They knew that the Halliwick House site within Friern had long been cherished by Haringey clinicians as a base for post-Friern services to the west of the borough; this no doubt influenced them in their recommendation that it should provide half the district's acute admission beds for the future. A development of eight houses forming a residential rehabilitation complex to be known as 'the Haven', and which was favoured by one of the consultant psychiatrists, was also to be placed on the Halliwick site.

Members of the feasibility group visited a day services unit at the Maudsley Hospital and a local authority workshop and day centre in Camden and felt that these facilities offered suitable prototypes for Haringey. A large hospital hostel development for the new long-stay population was planned for the St Ann's site, with nursing homes to provide for the majority of psychogeriatric patients and the 'old long-stay' patients. It was judged that a small proportion of the former group would be candidates for rehabilitation, and they were to be housed in slightly more ambitious social services schemes in the community. 'In the end', the DMO commented,

> to get out a timely document, a core group, or caucus formed. . . . The absence of psychiatrists is notable. By June [1983] we had produced a document agreed by the DHA, but disputed hotly by the consultants, partly through pique and partly through our refusal to plan for the part of the traditional catchment outside the Haringey boundary.[26]

But the very caution of this first Haringey plan drew forth a fairly withering response from the regional nurse planner: 'Not a very prepossessing document, not innovative at all, what a pity', she commented.

Then, in their attempts to implement the strategy, Haringey planners and managers found themselves blocked in several directions. Despite their concern that responsibility for the Halliwick site at Friern should pass to them for development, the RHA supported Hampstead's case, as managing district, to be the site developer. This meant that all the Haringey proposals had to be agreed through Hampstead-led project teams and accord with Hampstead proposals for retrenchment of Friern. To the east, the non-participation of the Claybury consultant psychiatrists, and the active opposition to reprovision of some of their colleagues at St Ann's made it difficult to plan at the more detailed level of specific projects, since some form of patient assessment information was felt to be required. In Waltham Forest the consultants' stance did not prevent detailed planning since nursing staff working for the district had extensive knowledge of patients in Claybury. Haringey planners lacked this information. Despite these difficulties for a time, during what could be seen as heady days in 1985, it seemed as if Haringey, improbably given its earlier repute within NETRHA, would become a site for major new initiatives and a shift to preventive styles of service. In the absence of psychiatrists and of any other key district team officers, the DMO led a planning team with wide membership. The team gave particular prominence to proposals for community mental health centres, crisis intervention teams and refuge houses. But in this enterprise much depended on the energy of the district medical officer and, to a certain extent, his ambition over-reached itself. Without access to a corporate member level group, he was also bereft of support from colleagues within the DMT such as the treasurer and the director of works.

One major project which was carried forward at this stage, the Grange project, was nurtured by the principal development officer in the social services department, the late Geoff Bromley. On both personal and professional levels he was highly committed to reprovision, as shown by his drafting of the first Haringey *DHA* plan submitted to the RHA. The Grange project was to be sited in a disused council building, which happened to be one of the few Georgian properties still standing in the borough and which possessed a number of striking architectural period features. It was to provide twelve residential and twenty-four day centre places for reprovision. Sadly Geoff Bromley's sponsorship of this scheme was brought to an end when he suffered a long illness that eventually led him to resign from the social services department.

Once the development officer became ill, the low level of interest in mental health among his senior colleagues within the council was exposed. The social services department could not even manage to respond formally to the district medical officer's consultative document in which he set out radically revised 'public health' model proposals which were far removed from the earlier hospital centred caution.

The other difficulty for the DHA in this period was that it had to counter deep popular suspicion of its intentions with regard to closure. As one veteran councillor complained about the prospects for the future of the smaller DGH site, St Ann's:

> Apathy is setting in. We fought for the Prince of Wales [hospital], where did that get us? People are fed up with the dictatorial way hospitals are being closed.

When DHA proposals for the development of St Ann's as a 'Centre for Health Care' became the subject of public consultation in 1987, only a handful of people could be attracted to the DHA's open public meetings.

Four voluntary organizations did, however, become involved in the DMO's planning team of twenty-four members in quite major ways. The participation of the PRA and MIND in Haringey centred chiefly upon proposals for group homes to be provided as part of the resettlement process. Two other organizations – Dalco and the Arbours Association – took up a more general advisory role: they might or might not be able to offer a service. The DHA did not keep to any consistent view of what it might expect of the voluntary sector, tending to be reactive rather than proactive.

Some way into the planning process, important differences of view emerged between the Haringey social workers based at Friern and their colleagues based in the borough headquarters at Wood Green. The former group felt that the local authority should be opposing the institutional type of Haringey plan that the use of Halliwick Hospital entailed at Friern. This would have been in line with the social services approach taken in Islington discussed earlier. But within the departmental headquarters the 'new Friern' complex had not aroused such concern. Some headquarters officers felt that reprovision offered the chance for extension of more traditional sheltered provision, such as adult fostering. Others felt that these traditions should be left behind since they did not offer enough opportunity for patients to exercise choice and to have the option of more independent accommodation. These differences came to the fore at a planning meeting in 1985, when the DHA was accused by an assistant director of the social services department of, in effect, ghettoizing patients by prepackaging shelter.

> The grouping of the needs of patients into three dependency categories without reference to the individual needs and desires of the people for whom we are planning is highly disturbing. . . .
>
> There seems to be an expectation that the social services department will provide personnel to assess the 'dependency' levels of patients within the hospitals and that small groups can be subsequently moved into the preselected accommodation 'in the community' as they come on stream, or into the adult care scheme.
>
> At the same time I believe that nursing staff in the hospitals are being given to understand that they will move into the community with the patients. Thus we will create the very situation we say we are trying to avoid – that of 'wards in the community'.

This intervention surprised the DMO, who felt that his fairly open-ended means of planning created the possibility for a wide range of schemes to be put forward. He was attempting to use the action space afforded by the absence of psychiatrists, and the support given to planning by Geoff Bromley's work, to forge alliances which enabled crisis intervention proposals to be piloted in the district (though he did not disavow the validity of hospital treatment). It was the DMO's view that Haringey ought to plan within the same framework as the neighbouring City and Hackney DHA, from within the borders of which patients had not been admitted to a long-stay hospital for more than ten years. Such an approach meant a reconceptualization of planning. One had to start by imagining that planning as if the Friern and Claybury transfer did not exist. Armed with a complete plan for that proportion of the Haringey population who would become ill in the future, the DHA could then 'fit' its Friern and Claybury population into the facilities required to achieve the model district service.

The ambitions of the DMO were aimed at achieving a service more revolutionary than that which was being developed almost simultaneously in Torbay. The focus on new admissions to the service being co-ordinated at community mental health centres was of particular interest, since it was planned for them to operate a bed bureau, a function previously seen as a hospital prerogative. At the largest of the centres it was planned to maintain the administrative headquarters of the mental health service. Given the far-reaching implications of these proposals, the RHA was happy to see district officers set the pace of change.

The psychiatrists' role in this phase of public health planning was to participate only through the mediation of a senior clinical officer at St Ann's, who described himself as a go-between in the process. In what was a system of 'virtual representation' of medical officers, the senior social workers and the CHC secretary were ranged, along with the DMO, on the opposite side of the planning divide. Nursing representatives passively accepted the public health approach while being more concerned with clarifying the structure of high dependency houses (the core houses or nursing homes, noted in Table 9) for the long-stay population in which their own profession would be providing the care.

Despite the fact that he worked hard to win acceptance for his public health approach to reprovision, which was developed collaboratively with some of the social service officers, the CHC and the voluntary organizations, the DMO alienated too many in the planning process. He had shifted policy-making too far from the earlier Haringey stance in favour of cautious reform of hospital centred services.

Both the DGM (appointed after the Griffiths reorganization) and the director of estates were not convinced that the plan had been fully thought through. The DGM was in any case being strongly lobbied by the psychiatrists. They had united across the hospitals to draw up a formal response to the DMO's consultative document announcing the public health model. They contested two fundamental assumptions which they believed were being made by the public health lobby.

1 that lay people could assess psychiatric conditions
2 that rehabilitation could be carried out entirely in residential settings.

Rather than just nursing homes, an additional ward at the St Ann's site would be required, which could be looked after by a proposed community psychiatrist.

In the end, partly as a result of the psychiatrists' opposition the community mental health centres were not pushed to the front of the reprovision implementation queue, as the DMO had wanted. The plan for admissions to be coordinated from a CMHC bed bureau was dropped.

This debate must be seen in a wider Haringey perspective, however. If the DMO's proposals were radical, they were certainly not received as such by some community groups. The proposals of the consultative document were roundly condemned by the 'Black Health Workers and Patients' Group', which had prepared a detailed response. The group stated that

> The lack of consultation with black groups during the research, plan-ning and formulative stages of the [consultative] document, merits protest in the strongest terms possible. Although working parties had met two years hence, including organizations such as MIND, to for-mulate the base of this document, Blacks were effectively excluded up until the 16 July, when they demanded circulation of this docu-ment, during a meeting with the CHC.

Of the community mental health centres, they went on to comment that

> Institutionalization is now to be transferred to community based centres. To eliminate stigma, psychiatric services must effectively integrate with general services. A building predominantly frequented by psychiatric staff and patients will inevitably become stigmatised, thus becoming symbolic of abnormalities.

Under their commentary on day care the group argued strongly that health authorities would have to adopt educational programmes to combat racist practices in the NHS:

> 'Racism Awareness Training' does not actively, or meaningfully, equip anyone to combat racism. For many it's just an academic ex-ercise. Being aware of racism is not equal to non-racism.
>
> Given that the society in which we live is racist, then resocial education, in relation to black patients, must be accorded greater consideration, with appropriate action, if Health Authorities are to provide a balanced service through policies, approaches, attitudes and influences.[27]

This was an important document, highlighting the apparent inability of the DHA to relate to organized community groups, and the lack of re-sponse of professional care staff to public concerns. It showed how much, with all the radicalism of the DMO, Haringey was very much a 'would-be guided' type of authority. Would-be because the guide-book exponent, the DMO, in this instance did not receive sufficient support from his col-leagues in the key professions, and nor from the top of the office. For the participation of local people in planning to occur, the DHA would have needed to display autarchic or decentralist features. Historically and corp-orately, it was not able to do this. Relating to the community was thus felt to be something which the CHC and possibly the Community Relations

Council laid on. Though the DHA appointed an ethnic development worker in 1986 with charity funding, in order to change its practices, this worker found it a difficult enough task simply to convince DHA officers that they themselves, white as they might be, should internalize and practise values of equal opportunity. Too often liaising with the black communities in the borough was seen as 'her department'.

The criticism by the Black Health Workers and Patients' Group therefore had potentially far-reaching implications. If services were to change in becoming more responsive and enabling to ethnic minority needs, then the task was surely something to be undertaken in Haringey even if it were not in any of the other Friern and Claybury catchment areas. The critique was one of the few from beyond the limited network of mental health specific agencies. It demonstrated how far removed the professional planning process was, even at its most 'public-friendly', lit by the gas lamp of a local community centre, from the forms of participation which consumer groups might have in mind.

No sooner had consultation on the DMO's mental health plan been carried out, than co-ordination of the affairs of the Haringey DHA began to suffer from some disruption, while the first of Sir Roy Griffiths's NHS reforms, general management, was implemented. The creation of a new organizational structure and of posts to staff meant an inevitable interregnum between the old regime and the new. This served only to increase the anxiety of the local authority, of housing associations and of voluntary organizations about the future of mental health provision. Rumours abounded, some to the effect that general managers would not be interested in anything other than decanting Claybury and Friern patients and that the mental health centres so prized by the DMO would be downgraded, if not cut altogether. There was a feeling that everything was being done behind closed doors and that the new atmosphere, post-general management, was not one conducive to partnership between the DHA and the other sectors.

There was good reason for this concern. The lack of involvement in mental health planning of the top-level finance, works and management staff of the DHA, set against the background of its corporate weakness, lent a little fragility and even implausibility to reprovision proposals as they stood in 1986. Midway through the year, when a new community and mental health services manager had become acquainted with the planned developments, he told a meeting of the joint consultative committee:

> When I arrived, I said this is the Haringey plan, can we afford it? No one said we could. We've got a mixture of early schemes which have been costed and others. I'm still optimistic that with the total available we can certainly transfer patients and provide CMHCs, beyond that we're into problem areas.

Supported by his DGM, the new manager was keen to work with the local authority, but always asking the question 'What would the local authority be doing if the DHA was not reproviding?' In other words to point out that the DHA expected some financial contribution from the local authority toward the cost of supporting the community mental health services consequent upon the closure of Friern and Claybury. Others involved in planning felt that a comprehensive inter-agency service could be purchased entirely out of the NHS's own Friern and Claybury reprovision money.

The net result of the general management approach was to induce a similar kind of pulling back from adjustment by appeal to symbolic normative values as had been a feature in Islington. Planning was recast around the *known* needs of the elderly Friern and Claybury inpatients. The putative needs of future non-asylum-resident users in the district, which the DMO had wished to see central to planning, were left as just that, putative, and therefore as something which did not need to be responded to in the immediate future. The public health model faded into the background, and with it the DMO. In common with many of his community physician colleagues up and down the country, he lost a considerable amount of power through the management reorganization and eventually left the district.

Just as this DHA review of prospects was being undertaken, the local authority, after a year and a half in which its contribution to planning had been somewhat slight, was beginning to develop a set of coherent mental health policies. Following the elections of 1986, a health committee was set up within the council, to co-ordinate its activity on health matters, and to put right its poor record on responding to proposals emerging from the rapidly changing NHS. Partly as a result of this improved focus on health, the local authority began to take up some of the criticisms of DHA plans which had surfaced earlier in the comments about dependency, selection and patient choice of the assistant director. As one of his senior social work colleagues, who felt deeply about the whole issue, put it: 'Finally someone was prepared to stand up and say we don't actually like this [Halliwick Haven] idea.'

Council members now launched a campaign through the joint consultative committee to get the long-stay provision for the west of the borough provided away from the Friern site. They felt that the Halliwick provision 'disenfranchised' Haringey residents, being situated outside the borough, and was too much oriented toward psychiatrists' needs for the continuation of Friern, albeit on a smaller scale.

By coincidence, and unknown to the local authority, the Halliwick complex was also facing hazards within the regionally co-ordinated project management process for its development. This was in part because of the complexity of the planning issues and in part because of the different interests in the site of Hampstead as manager of Friern, and Haringey as prospective principal user.

By 1987 the schemes planned for Halliwick were proving exorbitantly expensive in capital terms. While building cost inflation from 1983 was beginning to eat into the capital sum made available for reprovision, also in evidence was DHA 'bidding up' to the region, for what the RNO described as 'gold-plated' facilities. Costs were unacceptable to the RHA and the delays consequent upon this problem led the project architect to resign. Haringey officers were asked to reconsider the Halliwick concept and, if necessary, to look for alternatives.

This was a particularly unwelcome blow for the DHA. On Halliwick had turned the involvement in, and support for, reprovision of a consultant psychiatrist, who was chairman of the Friern medical committee. If the scheme were to be dropped, then there would certainly be a new wave of dissent from reprovision on the part of psychiatrists at Friern. Given that the local authority had changed its attitude toward the planned sheltered accommodation on the Halliwick site, and was now opposing it, DHA officers felt that their colleagues at the RHA were placing them in an embarrassing position. For they could apparently no longer rely on the support of the RHA in defending the Halliwick complex on the grounds that there was a clinical need for it. Changes in personnel at the region meant that its officers were moving towards a more equivocal position on Haringey's planning. Once again this was due to their perception that it had an 'institutional feel' to it. They were taking up the same critical stance as they had toward Waltham Forest's plans. A final twist to this tale was that the Service Manager for Mental Health in Haringey, appointed as part of the final round of the Griffiths general management reorganization in the district, was herself unhappy with the concept of the Halliwick development.

This withdrawal of support for Halliwick led the DHA to propose some reductions in the accommodation and facilities that would be provided. In the revised submissions to the RHA, existing buildings on the site were to be refurbished, in order to cut down on capital costs. Yet, after nearly four years of negotiation, finally, in December 1990, the DHA decided not to go ahead with the scheme at all.

This was an unexpected outcome, for the decision of the RHA to only partially close Friern in 1983 had rested on the Haringey case that the site was eminently suited to providing services for the west of the district. The development of the rehabilitation houses on the site was so much taken for granted, that the main efforts of housing associations and voluntary organizations in the borough were directed towards making sure that additional non-Friern services would also be set up as part of reprovision. In 1986, they proposed that a consortium be set up between the local authority, health authority and themselves which would develop a comprehensive range of mental health facilities in the district. Meetings were arranged of a group

> started in some despair by housing associations in order to get some idea of what was happening. They were worried that there would be

two kinds of care in the community developing – a local authority/
housing association type and a health authority type built on the
'medical model'. There were some good voluntary organisations
working in this field in Haringey and a combined strategy from both
housing associations and voluntary organisations would be a big
advantage.[28]

The appeal to the health authority of this proposition was that a consortium, as a charity, could draw on capital and revenue sources which the
DHA could not. For housing associations it offered the possibility to *participate* in planning and ensure that the process did not, under general management, simply revolve around the reprovision of Friern and Claybury.
Given a consortium with power-sharing, the potential for the DHA to shed
some of its institutional dominance was opened up by this proposal. The
membership structure was to be designed so that black and ethnic minority groups could play a prominent role. There was also believed to be a role
for the consortium in 'removing the political confrontation between the
health authority and the local authority'. For the council's housing adviser:

This was vital – the housing department were desperate to reduce
spending on Bed and Breakfast, which was 'home' to a large number
of mentally vulnerable people.[29]

The joint consultative committee at length agreed eleven aims for the
consortium, ranging from 'planning development and management of
housing and support services for the mentally ill' through 'monitoring the
development and provision of mental health services by all agencies', to
'providing a platform for expressing an independent view as to their ade-
quacy and relevance'.

Nevertheless, to get the secure agreement for the establishment of the
consortium, the associations had to accept reprovision as its *short-term*
goal, and only a small portion of reprovision at that – twenty-eight places
within the resettlement programme. This was in line with the views of
the new general manager for the community units in Haringey who considered that planning would have to concentrate on the specific needs of
Friern and Claybury resident patients. The consortium's objective of a
comprehensive inter-agency range of services potentially deviated from
such a focus, and, in the view of the general manager, it could probably
not be addressed until the Friern and Claybury resettlement programme
was nearing completion.

Conclusion

Haringey was the least likely place for a 'community-owned' strategy to
emerge. Planning began in the midst of a number of extremely un-
propitious circumstances. The record of the outgoing district officers in

1982 was the subject of some criticism. The birth-pangs of the new DHA, torn from the womb of the Enfield and Haringey Area Health Authority, were such that the infant body appeared to have a limited life in prospect. With half of the district area served by a neighbouring health authority and no central general hospital site to serve as a focus for development within its boundaries, the new authority was ripe for mergers in the minds of more powerful teaching authorities for example.

At the same time there was a major issue about whether any DHA, let alone Haringey, could achieve the scale of planning which reprovision, by catchment area accident, imposed upon it. Whether a DHA would have the officer capacity to work from both the hospitals which were being closed and prepare plans for such a large number of patients, around 440, was open to question. If senior officers of the district management team in the key professions had wished to make this their central task, there was a possibility that it might be brought off. But with the general management reform intervening in the process of change, and with a divided authority at the level of members presiding over planning, that was not in prospect.

That the DHA managed to put plans together was in itself something of an achievement. Without the early efforts of the DMO and of Geoff Bromley from the social services department, it is conceivable that the RHA might have decided to give the west of the district to Islington for making mental health provision, and the Edmonton borough to Enfield, leaving just the east of the district for Haringey to serve itself. This would have reduced the management task and recognized the difficulties faced by the DHA in establishing its viability.

DHA planners were also faced with a situation in which the majority of consultant psychiatrists responsible for patients from the district, whether at Friern, Claybury or St Ann's, were not supportive of reprovision. This meant that the platform from which the DMO operated was weakened considerably, and that much rested on keeping the support of the consultant champion of the Halliwick project and on widening the ownership of planning within the district management team. These were the necessary conditions for a guided method of reprovision.

If there was one area where a sustained community development strategy would be required to get input from the local population into planning it was Haringey. Yet with the disunity of the health authority and its fragility, it would be difficult to envisage any such programme being devised, still less embarked upon. There was little evidence that the DHA would be able to adopt autarchic procedures for its mental health policy making. The most that could be expected would be that professional innovators might on their own account attempt to involve 'the community' in an ad-hoc fashion. The consortium carried within it possibilities for a change to this situation but was given a marginal role restricted to reprovision.

Overview of the response from the localities to the NETRHA closure decision

Early plans of the three DHAs were based on technical discretionary judgements of professional carers about the dependency and needs of the resident populations of Friern and Claybury. In Islington, a Consultant Psychiatrist, together with psychologists and senior social services officers, played a major role in preparing proposals and setting down guidelines for the kind of resettlement that would be acceptable. In Waltham Forest, the Director of Nursing at Claybury, supported by colleagues within the mental health unit, and again, in consultation with senior social services officers, took a leading part in the development of the 'reprovision' plan. In Haringey, non-expert officers in both the DHA and the Local Authority sought advice from expert opinion in psychiatry and studied developments in community services in order to produce a plan. They were assisted by 'hesitant supporters' amongst the psychiatrists.

These judgements were then opened up to adjustment as the long-term planning process became established. DHA adjustment to the proposals of outside agencies was particularly marked in Islington, where an informed network of activists was prominent on the CHC, within voluntary organizations, and on the Borough Council's mental health committee. In Haringey and Waltham Forest on the other hand, the process of adjustment was largely one of negotiation between groups of professional staff *within* the respective DHAs. In Haringey the DMO's strong advocacy of a public health model led to much planning team work being carried out on the community mental health centres. At the same time, most consultant psychiatrists providing services to the district disputed the validity of the model. The DMO did not enjoy support from all those of his senior colleagues who would be significant figures in the implementation of the DHA plan. Initially the Borough Council displayed little interest in the debate and the network of voluntary organization activists was much more dispersed than in Islington. Later, the Council became more involved, as did housing associations, and their collaboration with the DHA in the founding of a consortium of mental health agencies, held the promise of Health Authority adjustment to the demands of the non-statutory sector. Partly because of the underlying organizational weakness of Haringey DHA, the promise was not fulfilled.

In Waltham Forest, the voluntary sector, the Borough Council and the CHC played a very minor role in the process of development of the DHA plan for reprovision. At an early stage the Local Authority assigned the task of resettlement of long-stay patients to the health authority. They agreed with mental health unit officers that reprovision was primarily a health care task. Most Senior District managers chose not to get involved in the issue and, under pressure of the withdrawal from planning of their consultant psychiatrists, the DHA adopted a cautious plan in which the first loyalty was seen to be that owed to Claybury patients. Later, District and RHA managers became concerned about the lack of priority given to community needs and to the integration of psychiatry with other medical services offered in Waltham Forest. The mental health unit was thus forced from the top, not from the outside, to adjust its planning.

Islington displayed many of the characteristics of an autarchic authority but resisted the proposals for decentralization of decision making presented by the voluntary organizations. Haringey DHA had history, and the sheer number of people whom it had to resettle from the two hospitals, against it. At the same time, it was an organization whose viability was constantly in jeopardy. Those officers leading the reprovision initiative had to seek for guidance where they could find it, as many of those who would be implementing plans were not committed to them. Whilst some proposals were made later in the planning process to consult with carers' and relatives' groups, and to support users, the scale of work required, especially to work with ethnic minority organizations, was too formidable in such a situation. Waltham Forest chose not to interpret the Claybury decision as an opportunity to realize objectives for the creation of a comprehensive, inter-agency service in the district, and acquiesced to the mental health unit's position that resources would only allow for hospital reprovision. That reprovision would be centred on health care with the NHS playing the major role. The unit thus acted in many ways as a reluctant arm of the centre.

With the three authorities tending to be controlled, guided or tending to strive to autarchy, rather than to follow a decentralized or Athenian pattern of action, the technical judgements of professional carers were given much weight. In all welfare issues there is a tension between legal obligations, professional advice, and consumer choice, as is clear in the theoretical framework outlined in Chapter 3. In the early 1980s it was simply thought an impractical proposition, for planning purposes, to involve long stay mental hospital residents in the decision-making for the development of new placements. The interaction of authority behaviour with this underlying view from within psychiatry, had an important impact on the outcome for people leaving hospital.

References

1 NETRHA (1983). *Report to the Regional Health Authority on Feasibility Studies on Mental Illness Services in the Catchment Areas of Claybury and Friern Hospitals*. London, NETRHA.
2 Bromley, G. (1984). Hospital closure: death of institutional psychiatry? University of Essex, unpublished dissertation, MA in Social Services Planning, p. 66.
3 National Schizophrenia Fellowship (1989). *Slipping Through the Net*, Surbiton, Concern Communications.

4 Bachrach, P. and Baratz, M.S. (1970). *Power and Poverty: Theory and Practice*, New York, Oxford University Press.

5 Islington Health Authority (1983). *Report on Review of Acute Services*, April, para 10f, London, Islington Health Authority.

6 Hodge, M. (1987). When tomorrow comes, *New Socialist* January, 36–8.

7 DHSS (1974). *Collaboration between Health and Local Authorities*, NHS Reorganization Circular HRC (74) 19, London, DHSS.
DHSS (1976). *Joint Care Planning: Health and Local Authorities*, Health Circular HC (76) 18, London, DHSS.
DHSS (1983). *Care in the Community and Joint Finance*, Health Circular HC (83) 6, London, DHSS.

8 DHSS (1983).

9 London Borough of Islington Social Services Committee (1984). *Islington District's Psychiatric Service to Replace Friern Hospital – Alternative Draft Capital Plan*. 27 February, London, Borough of Islington.

10 Minutes of the NETRHA meeting, 25 July 1983.

11 London Borough of Waltham Forest Social Services Committee (1984). *Waltham Forest Joint Consultative Committee: Proposals to Improve Consultation*, 1 February, London, Borough of Waltham Forest.

12 London Borough of Waltham Forest Social Services Committee (1985). *Policy Review 1986/7*, 24 October, London, Borough of Waltham Forest.

13 Interview with the author, 7 March 1985.

14 ibid.

15 Consultant Psychiatrists' Critique (undated). *Claybury Hospital Reprovision – Proposals by the Claybury Medical Hospital Staff*, circulated January 1986.

16 ibid.

17 ibid.

18 ibid.

19 ibid.

20 ibid.

21 McMahon, L. and Blunden, R. (1989). *Review of the Forest Community Project: an Interim Report for the Waltham Forest Joint Consultative Committee, Sub Committee on the Forest Community Project*, September, London, Borough of Waltham Forest.

22 Griew, A. (1984). *Mental Health Planning in Haringey: a Brief Outline of the Process – July 1982 to August 1984*, para 3, document circulated internally.

23 Bromley (1984), p. 62.

24 ibid., pp. 76–7.

25 ibid., p. 84.

26 Griew (1984), para. 4.

27 Black Health Workers and Patients' Group (1985). *Response to Consultative Document of Haringey Health Authority: a Comprehensive District Based Service for Mentally Ill People in Haringey and Edmonton*, September, London, Black Health Workers and Patients' Group.

28 Notes of Care in the Community Mental Health Group, 16 January 1987.

29 Minutes of the Community Mental Health Services Meeting between representatives of Haringey Care in the Community Mental Health Group and Haringey Health Authority officers, 20 March 1987.

6

What happened to the patients?

There are difficulties about treating the reprovision of the large psychiatric hospitals as a test of community care. To an extent, the institutions built away from the large cities have already become integrated with residential communities that have since been created around them. Few wards or areas within the hospitals are locked and they are open for patients and visitors alike to come and go without restriction. When looking at some of the aims of reprovision programmes, to enable residents to manage money, shop and use public transport, this is an important point to bear in mind. The plans for their closure have not been subject to the kind of large scale public opposition which district health authorities have faced when proposing to close local acute hospitals practising general medicine. However, the mental hospitals often do not lack for supporters in the residential communities which surround their perimeters. When the NETRHA set out to establish the feasibility of closing Friern and Claybury in 1982, the Rector for Friern, Barnet collected more than fifty signatures from his congregation to a petition urging the improvement and extension of the services of Friern.[1]

There were also aspects of the process of change which would lead to an expectation that problems of adjustment which patients may experience can be seen as 'natural' or 'normal'. Given the commonly long periods of residence in hospital it would be surprising if the experience of moving home did not cause a certain amount of distress to those resettled. The uprooting from friendship and acquaintanceship networks in which patients may have been comfortable, if not content, has received little attention. Any transition of this kind brings with it a sense of loss and unfamiliarity for those resettled, together with a fear that they may not fit into the culture of the new neighbourhood.

Other factors which complicate the assessment of community care are the staff–patient and staff–resident relationships. Perring, in her anthropological study of the development of two group homes in the Friern and Claybury catchment areas, argues that these homes continue to carry 'benign' forms of authority like those found in the psychiatric hospital.[2] While there are staff provided to supervise residents, and the latter group are not being thrown back on to family and friends, this mode of reprovision removes the possibility for reciprocity. Instead the group home functions in a 'quasi-familial' manner in which staff take the role of the parents and the residents that of the children. This is despite the fact that though 'the nuclear family remains the model for family life in Britain, . . . single parent or "serial" families are becoming more common and are less likely to be regarded as "deviant" '.[3]

Godin's study of staff attitudes at another Claybury reprovision project tends, on the whole, to bear out the contention that group homes have these built-in, quasi nuclear-familial, assumptions. Attempting to develop 'personal constructs', following Kelly's theory, he asked each member of staff to describe 'how they were to the residents' and 'how the residents were to them'.[4] In terms of how they perceived 'staff to residents' relations the staff offered a number of descriptions such as 'mothering, parenting, nurse, directive, adviser, caring, fatherly', to which corresponded aspects of the 'residents to staff' relations such as 'little girl wanting affection, perceives me as a nurse, trusts, confiding, respects, looks to me for understanding'. Nevertheless, one or more of the residents was considered 'grandfatherly' towards staff and friendship or friendliness was reciprocal.

The most notable feature of the list of concepts held was that negative attitudes of the relationships such as being indifferent, disliking, insulting, rejecting, condescending, were all listed on the resident-to-staff side. Staff did not indicate that they themselves held any reciprocal attitudes of a negative kind.

The TAPS study

In making the decision to close Friern and Claybury, the RHA decided that the implementation of the resettlement process should be the subject of independent evaluation, given its novelty for an urban area with the problems of London. The Team for Assessment of Psychiatric Services (TAPS), led by Professor Julian Leff, a psychiatrist, was set up in 1985 to assess the outcome for every long-stay patient leaving each of the hospitals. At a census date in 1985, more than 800 patients fell within the criteria for the study. The criteria were (1) a length of stay in hospital of one year or more, and (2) in the case of patients over 65 years old, a primary diagnosis which was not dementia. New patients continued to be added to the 'baseline' list of 1985 as they stayed over the 'trigger point' of one year. All patients were to be assessed before leaving hospital and then reassessed after one year of residence in the community.[5]

A range of different measures of patient characteristics was devised which would be sensitive to changes significant from medical, psychological and social points of view. Some of these were based on well-established questionnaires, such as the 'Present State Examination' by which psychiatrists attempt to complete a symptom count from the presence of delusions and other manifestations of, at its crudest, madness in the interlocutor. The 'Patient Attitude Questionnaire' asked patients/ residents about their likes and dislikes concerning their placement and care, and perception of changes in themselves. They were also asked about the nature and extent of their social contacts. Carers were interviewed to get an idea of the social adeptness and domestic skills of their clients, and the different rules and regulations of the hospital and community settings were compared. In order to test whether changes in patients'/residents' conditions in the community were simply an effect of rehabilitation that would have happened in hospital anyway, 'leavers' were 'matched' as far as possible for diagnosis, age, social problems, and length of stay, with a control group of patients who were likely to remain in hospital until later in the rundown process.

Anderson, Dayson and Wills of TAPS reported in 1989, after the first 161 patients in the study who had left hospital had been assessed, that

> The most striking feature of the analysis is that we could detect no difference in clinical, social behavioural, or social network outcomes between hospital matches and leavers who had spent one year in the community.[6]

This finding was confirmed in the two following years, 1990 and 1991, when TAPS reported that across all the main variables – symptomatology, social behaviour, domestic skills and social networks – for the 357 leavers who had been assessed after one year in the community, 'there were no significant differences in the changes in the leaver group compared with changes in the matched group'.[7]

These findings appear to suggest that patients moving out of hospital do not become any less 'mad' or any more 'able', at least in the clinician's view, one year after moving out to the community. But once resident in their community placements, 'leavers' very much preferred the setting to that of the hospital. These attitudes were not simply a consequence of negative views of the hospital left behind 'but represented an increased approval of their current setting'. There were fewer rules and regulations, standardized meal-times and so on, in the community, and the greater freedom conferred was often referred to in patients' own comments about their environment. But despite this consumer vote in favour of reprovision it appears tempered in the case of a large body of 'leavers' by a desire to 'move on' from their placements. Subsequent TAPS analysis of the views of a sample of 117 hospital leavers indicated that only half 'had no desire to move on from their present accommodation'. One-third of the sample, on the other hand, 'stated some desire not to remain permanently in the accommodation'. A substantial proportion of the group expressing this desire (43 per cent) wanted to move on to a home of their own.[8]

What was the character of the initial placements?

The planning process in Islington, Waltham Forest and Haringey, which was outlined in the previous chapter, illustrates that initial programmes for re-settlement to be concentrated in either general hospital wards or in nursing homes in the community gave way to a more mixed range of placements. The voluntary sector, housing associations and local authorities were to provide shelter for a significant proportion of the long-stay population.

NETRHA reprovision allowed for a total of 1,678 inpatient places, open to admissions in each hospital in 1983, to be re-established away from the two asylum sites within the ten-year programme. But the population of the hospitals was not, of course, static. Planned vacant bed levels and predic-tions as to the death-rate of elderly patients played a part in the calculation of the provision required. Short-stay admission wards accounted for a great deal of turnover, since patients were not normally expected to stay for longer than a period of two or three months. However, a number of such admissions did lead to patients staying longer than a year. At the same time, a minority of patients retained their own homes while in hospital. Sometimes they had lived in, and retained, council housing, sometimes they were owner-occupiers, and sometimes they had places within rela-tives' homes to which they desired to return. Therefore not all patients in the reprovision programme would be resettled in the new provision re-placing the wards of the hospital.

These aspects are reflected in the range of moves of the 278 patients who left Friern and Claybury between August 1985 and August 1988, and who were assessed by TAPS. The majority were resettled in staffed group homes and hostels. Most of these placements (143) were in schemes run either directly by health authorities, or financed as part of the reprovision programme. Others were in private homes which formed part of an established domestic economy around the large hospitals. One such home, consisting of two adjacent semi-detached properties, knocked together, was located only a few hundred yards from Friern. Providing for twelve patients, it was owned and operated by a married couple, each of whom had worked at Friern and one of whom continued to work there while playing a part in the operation of the home.

Around one in seven patients (thirty-eight) returned to their 'own homes', often council flats, or to live with relatives. Smaller numbers were placed in 'board-with care' schemes and in old people's homes. One-third of the provision within these latter schemes was in projects specifically dedicated to the hospital closure programme. The breakdown in relation to each of the three 'cohorts' analysed by TAPS is given in Figures 3 and 4.

Figure 3 Community facilities provided for patients in the first-year cohort of leavers

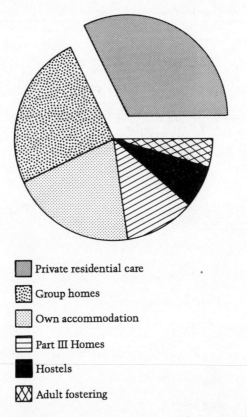

- ▨ Private residential care
- ▨ Group homes
- ▧ Own accommodation
- ☰ Part III Homes
- ■ Hostels
- ▨ Adult fostering

Source: From Dayson, D. (1990) in *Moving Long Stay Patients into the Community: First Results*, Proceedings of TAPS Fourth Annual Conference, London, NETRHA.

The fact that not all long-stay patients were placed in care homes directly funded from 'reprovision moneys' and organized to provide permanent shelter is at first sight disturbing. However, the TAPS analysis could throw up no significant differences between the outcome for people placed in these 'purpose-planned' facilities and that of the others spread across the more usual range of private care and publicly funded, but not mental health-specific, hostels. Only six patients appeared to have drifted into vagrancy, the team being unable to trace them at the time of follow-up, with three having already led a vagrant life-style before hospital admission. The choice of many 'leavers' to return to their 'own homes' was a positive one with which they were content. Were all long-stay patients, including the younger groups, to be pushed toward planned

Figure 4 Community facilities provided for patients in the second-year cohort of leavers

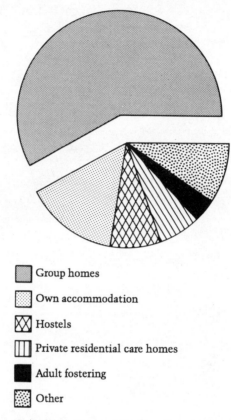

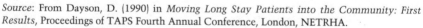

Group homes

Own accommodation

Hostels

Private residential care homes

Adult fostering

Other

Source: From Dayson, D. (1990) in *Moving Long Stay Patients into the Community: First Results*, Proceedings of TAPS Fourth Annual Conference, London, NETRHA.

separate provision, a mass transfer into institutional care would be in prospect.

The group homes and hostels organized to replace hospital care for most of the long-stay patients usually took the form of 'ordinary' houses acquired in residential neighbourhoods. Occasionally, homes which had previously served as staff accommodation and which were already in NHS ownership were commandeered for the reprovision programme. Although many placements were still to take the form of purpose-built sheltered schemes which would in effect, be nursing homes, these dwellings, with one exception, had not been constructed by 1988 (see Figure 5). The one exception provided for twenty-four residents and thirty-five day hospital attenders. The residential part of the scheme was made up of three

Figure 5 The shape of the future: design for a purpose-built sheltered scheme to be run by nursing staff

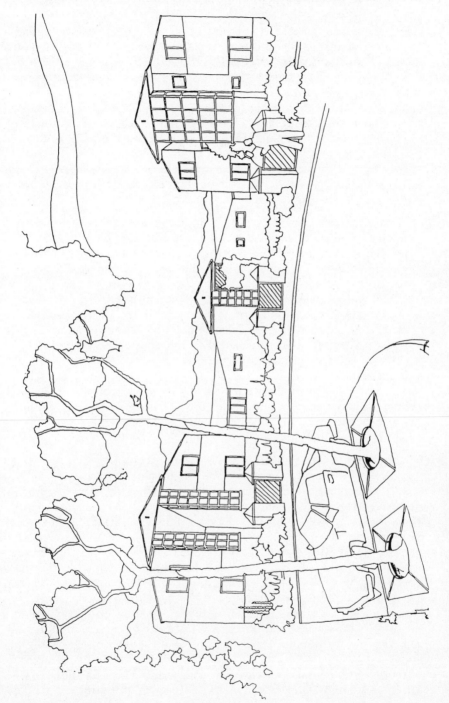

Source: Roger Parkin of TANGRAM Associates.

eight-person houses, each 'with staff present at all times, set around a central courtyard with landscaping, trees and a pedestrian access' and designed to 'function independently [from the hospital estate where they were situated] to the extent that each will have a street number and receive normal postal and milk deliveries'.

The houses were of 'typical Scandinavian design . . . craftsmen built and assembled on site under the supervision of the Danish manufacturer', their overall appearance therefore being of 'a high-quality private residential development'.

The typical very large but 'ordinary' houses, acquired specially to form reprovision hostels, presented something of a contrast. One such house was described in the following terms

> The hostel is situated in a pleasant, quiet residential area within easy reach of local shops, bus and tube routes . . . the building itself looks much like other houses in the vicinity – large semi-detached and well maintained. The two neighbours' buildings are both private residential houses. . . .
>
> The building has four floors. The basement contains a large kitchen, a large dining room, a utility room with a washing machine and drier, a toilet, a small store room with adjacent shower and a door leading to the garden path alongside the house. The ground floor contains the staff office where the files and medication are kept, a toilet and two large living rooms. The front room contains a television and a video, and the back room a stereo system. ... . The first floor contains another small staff office, a shower and toilet, one single [bed]room and two double rooms. The top floor has two bathrooms with toilets, one single room and three double rooms.

Smaller but still substantial houses were bought on the open market by some of the health authorities to serve for group homes staffed by nurses. One such home was visited by the author. It has the benefit of being situated close to a well-known and extensive north London park offering a number of facilities, and, like the above hostel location, is convenient for shops and bus routes. The house is detached, Victorian in design, and, like the hostel already described, extends over four floors. The kitchen, again in the basement, opens out into a large garden, which is, however, overlooked by a small block of flats next door. There is a large detached dwelling of a similar construction to the home on the other side. The house is well furnished with comfortable, non-institutional chairs and carpeting of places. The lounge areas are situated on the ground floor, the bedrooms on the first and second floors and the staff office on the top floor.

Another Victorian house, owned by a housing association and used for a MIND group home project which, like the health authority group home, functioned as a high-support facility where staff could 'sleep-in', appeared to give as high if not a higher standard of environment. A TAPS worker visiting the home after it had been open a year commented that

> The kitchen facilities in particular are very impressive. Each of the six residents is allocated their own fridge and cupboard space, both of which are colour coded and provided with padlocks. The level of equipment – oven, microwave, utensils, etc. was the highest I had seen during the year and the bedrooms and sitting room were also very well kitted out. Each resident had their own single room and these were fairly spacious.

However, these alternatives to hospital were not always so immune from criticism. One of a number of houses run with peripatetic support from a voluntary sector group was described as 'a fairly dirty, neglected looking building from the outside', with this impression being largely confirmed for the observer as true of the inside as well:

> There were two men living in the part of the house I visited and they were living in fairly, but not very squalid conditions . . . the kitchen in particular was very messy. . . . Overall I was not very impressed with the facilities available

A health authority hostel was also roundly criticized by one of the professional carers working there, because in its first year

> some parts of the house were extremely dirty. Some residents and staff suffered from stomach infections which might well have been due to low levels of cleanliness, and parts of the house were infested with flies.

A firm of professional cleaners subsequently had to be contracted to clean up the worst of the rooms.

These then were the settings of hospital replacement facilities. The TAPS interviews suggest that patients express a high degree of satisfaction with them. On what is this based?

Wills, Dayson and Gooch carried out analysis of the coded responses to the structured Patient Attitude Questionnaire given by 'leavers' in the first two years of the TAPS study.[9] They looked particularly at answers to the questions: 'What do you like about where you live?' and 'What do you dislike about where you live?' Answers had been rated by interviewers as falling into the following categories:

1 care-givers
2 company (fellow residents)
3 amenities
4 degree of permissiveness or lack of restrictions
5 general approval
6 nothing liked or disliked
7 unrateable response.

Broadly there was a significantly greater degree of liking for aspects of life outside hospital than for aspects of life inside it. Wills, Dayson and Gooch draw attention to residents' appreciation of the greater degree of permissiveness in the community. This appreciation points to the move out of hospital having a generalized 'liberating effect'.

Godin, in his interviews with residents at one of the first staffed group homes established out of Claybury, concluded that there were three main elements in the responses. First, 'the concept of freedom was used in a superordinate way to describe many of the positive benefits' of living in the project. These included the opportunity to decide for oneself what and when to eat, to wash personal clothing and to see to the general condition of the home (residents had responsibility for their 'own' houses, with one house of four in a terrace being the 'staff house'). They also included being more able generally to work things out and realize one's abilities, and having 'greater control and power over one's life'.[10]

This 'positive freedom' can also be identified as a central element in the views of Friern and Claybury patients discharged in the first three years of the programme.

One resident of an unstaffed MIND group home commented that

> you get on and do things yourself, make more friends, and invite people to dinner here and go to dinner there.

Another resident of the house run by the same team simply commented that she preferred the accommodation outside hospital because it gave freedom, gave opportunities for meeting people and was self-contained:

> I go out more, I see more of my own people, I visit more of my family, my sisters.

A patient who had moved back to his own home argued that

> There was a stigma associated with being in hospital. Now I have freedom, family life and can see friends . . . I'm far more confident and outward going. I can now be a useful member of society. I felt like I was a non-entity whilst I was at Claybury.

Many commented that they felt more confident after leaving hospital. A resident of a DHA hostel explained that he was 'happier and more confident, having experienced a healthy change'. He considered the reason for this change was 'being outside and mixing with people'.

The second of Godin's categories of responses in his interviews with community residents, he suggests are best considered as descriptions of 'negative freedom'. This meant for residents,

> being free of a big institution in which one could 'get picked on', being free of disruption caused by sharing with disturbed patients, and being free to get up at night to make tea without 'being coaxed back to bed by the night nurse'.[11]

Although the distinction between positive and negative freedom is often not clear cut, the latter concept can also be identified in the perceptions of the leavers questioned by TAPS. Thus one (non-reprovision) hostel resident commented that

> There's more freedom, we can do what we like, I can have a nice bath, we can do everything when we want. There's no pressure on us in any way.

A 'leaver' in a voluntary sector home found that there was 'a very relaxed atmosphere' where he could 'make hot drinks day or night'. Another, living in a local authority hostel, stated that he had been

> fed up in hospital. Here, the nurses are not around you in white coats telling you to do this and that.

One person, who felt much happier and more confident in a council flat to which he had moved after hostel placement, commented that a major advantage of his accommodation was that there were no disturbed fellow residents. A woman resident at a voluntary sector group home stated that in Friern she could have no personal possessions since they would be destroyed and she thus found the privacy of the new home a very positive change.

As a third category of residents' attitudes, Godin refers to their complaints about the impositions of the new freedom, such as having to do housework. Again, this was also a major feature of the TAPS interviews. Thus one person readmitted to hospital after a period in a MIND group home stated that he

> couldn't cope with cleaning and cooking. It was terrible, the place was too small. I had to go out nearly every day to do shopping and so on.

Another resident of an NHS hostel was more vehement. The responses of this person were all accompanied by expletives. He used these to make the point in no uncertain terms that he and his fellow residents wanted 'a proper cook and cleaners', rather than be asked to help with domestic activity. Within a local authority hostel, a client reported 'being told to do the washing up' as a disadvantage of the placement.

On the other hand, a MIND group home tenant who stated that 'They pushed me out [from hospital] kindly', did not object to shopping and cooking but said that she missed being cooked for.

Having reached his late 70s, a resident in a health authority group home, while finding staff much better in the home and valuing the time they gave for talking, expressed his opposition to organized community activities in the following way: 'All I want to do is die and have a big wooden box.'

Further study of the comments recorded by various TAPS researchers, reveals that two additional categories of response can be drawn out. The first concerns complaints about money problems and the second centres upon the problems of tension with fellow residents, a sense of loss of the opportunity to meet with lots of other patients either at Friern or at Claybury and loneliness.

One tenant of a council flat said that ideally he would prefer to live in Eire if he had the money. For the moment he 'would like a cheap place to have tea and meet people in the evenings'. He also said that he was experiencing problems with claiming benefits. Another person occupying a council flat wanted more money so that he could travel to London. He said that his main 'difficulties in living' were 'getting the home set up, furniture and so on'.

A tenant occupying her own flat, listing 'desired activities' as 'dancing and parties', said that her main living problems arose from the fact that the previous year her cohabitee had not been receiving his benefits and was not able to pay his rent.

Regarding problems with other residents, one young resident in a MIND group home, who reported lots of positive things in the transition to the community, such as seeing his family more often and getting on better with them, said that there were, however,

> lots of rows, I usually have the last word, I have arguments with fellow residents, they're a pain in the head.

Despite this, he said that he had changed in his behaviour:

> I behave myself, I control my temper now, temper was my trouble.

One woman in a house forming part of the same project felt 'nervous' and did not get on with the two other women living there. Another resident in a rehabilitation hostel said that she had

> No peace, no friendship and little room. I row with everyone I don't like and they've gone.

A more ambivalent statement by a resident in one of the first voluntary sector group homes to be set up, while expressing the view that the house was too small for five residents and that the others were lazy with the housework, went on to talk about some of the facilities which Friern had offered and which, living in the community, she missed. She had attended painting and English lessons at the hospital and felt that painting made her well:

> It's more interesting in Friern, you meet new people all the time – new patients, staff, occupational therapists and the like. Here it's much more limited. There should be a good mental health day centre within walking distance.

Loneliness in the community was quite often mentioned. Not surprisingly it was chiefly described by those who were not in group homes or other house collectives. One council flat tenant, for instance, said that his difficulties in living were to do with 'health and noise'. He felt that his condition was deteriorating because of 'loneliness, stress and depression' as well as 'noise from above'. Another tenant who had friends at a local club also said that his health was getting worse and, asked to point to differences between his present accommodation and the hospital, said that he had 'made many friends in Friern'. Another person similarly placed in an independent flat said that although he had made a few friends in the community, he ascribed his loneliness to living on his own in the flat.

The brief comments of residents presented here have been drawn randomly from a mass of mostly coded responses to the structured Patient Attitude Questionnaire of TAPS. A much broader range of qualitative data was gathered in Perring's study of the reprovision process within specific local settings.

In fieldwork carried out in three voluntary sector group homes, she occupied a non-staff role somewhere between staff helper and confidante to residents. Her study, she argues,

> shows that the philosophy of the group home, and its practical running are grounded in kinship oriented assumptions. The group home, as a quasi familial home, within the voluntary organisation, is ideally visualised as the basis for a sort of alternative community.[12]

But it is also one which, 'because the voluntary organisation has not sought a way of reintegrating it' in the neighbourhood, remains 'isolated within the community'.[13]

As Perring came to know residents of the group homes, she began to appreciate that there were important details of their life histories which had remained neglected during their long tenures of 'patienthood' in the asylum. The extent of residents' family commitments was revealed. The significance of some residents' experience of evacuation from London in their youth, because of the danger of wartime bombing, became apparent. It is difficult to do justice to the rich narrative of Perring's work, but the following account of a significant life-event which was related to her by one resident illustrates the emotional suffering which some of the residents had earlier endured:

> I remember being in hospital when my son was born. I had to lie in bed with a glucose drip in my arm. I was very upset because the baby was taken off me and I heard the nurse shouting at him when he cried. It was very difficult to rest in there. He was a beautiful baby and I couldn't bear for him to be shouted at. I felt better when I got home. I called him Mark Thomas. I hoped that if I had another son I'd call him Thomas. I thought of adopting another one you know. I don't know where he is now.[14]

Details of such experiences were, Perring states, often not known by hospital staff, reflecting 'the lack of interest in the aspects of patients' lives which do not, from a clinical viewpoint, appear to relate to their patienthood'.[15]

One of the issues which the study highlights regarding the selection of patients for the projects is that the voluntary organization was not so much concerned with the level of domestic dependency of patients – how far they were able to wash and cook – so much as whether in their 'street behaviour' they would draw attention to themselves and become vulnerable to public ridicule. One patient was somewhat deaf and was sometimes shouted at because of this deafness. He also did not follow structured day care. Though a candidate favoured by staff to move in to one of the group homes, there was a long debate within the voluntary organization as to whether he would successfully settle in the community. As Perring puts it, the managers felt that he was unable to 'maintain face'.

Much importance was attached to the process of leaving and its emotional significance. This mainly centred upon visits to the houses, sometimes before any furniture or equipment had been delivered to them. Yet although there was preparation in the form of such visits, the act of leaving itself was played down by both hospital and resettlement staff. Perring points out that this constituted a denial of the 'rite of passage' which the transition represented. The consequence of such denial was that when patients faced problems in adapting to the new life, these tended to be approached as being attributable to illness. This was demonstrated by the fact that readmission to hospital or placement in provision offering more supervision outside the project would be a final resort in cases where the problem, be it depression, not eating, or unsociability and withdrawal, remained unsolved.

The playing-down of the event of leaving for one group of patients is recorded in the following way:

> The departure was very low key. (I recall it now as being almost silent, a rather dismal affair.) Most patients weren't on the ward anyway and the staff made minimal fuss. The sister passed their belongings down the fire escape (which provided a convenient point of access from the car park), calling a domestic worker to help her. The three residents helped, even though I was there to carry bags. They all ended up standing at the bottom of the fire escape, in the pouring rain. No one went back up and no one came out to say goodbye. There was no final wave. All three were due to revisit the hospital on Monday, to sort out financial matters, and Margaret and Hilda were expecting to return regularly to the workshop.[16]

When one of the 'leavers', Hilda, subsequently became 'unwell' the problem of such illness being considered against notions of patienthood was readily apparent. She had stopped attending the workshop, because she believed that one of the staff on the ward she had previously lived in disliked her, the proof of this being that the same sister had pushed her out by the back door – the fire escape.[17]

Citing Marris, Perring draws attention to the grieving process that may be expected to accompany such a major life-change as a move out of hospital. Although the home in hospital may not have been greatly valued and may have been associated with unhappiness, mourning over loss at the 'death' of the hospital could be seen as a natural reaction.

At this point it is important to sound a cautionary note about the representativeness of the groups of residents assessed by TAPS and those in whose resettlement Perring participated. In the Waltham Forest planning process discussed in Chapter 5, one of the chief concerns of the consultant psychiatrists at Claybury was that the more motivated and 'able' patients were being selected for the first reprovision projects. The remaining population thus consisted of a more withdrawn and disabled group who were being 'left behind'. Certainly David Jones, in analysing the Friern and Claybury populations, found evidence that those more articulate and interested in moving were being resettled early on. He found that

> Leavers are significantly younger than the remaining group and have spent significantly less time in hospital. [They] are less likely to have a diagnosis of schizophrenia . . . have significantly fewer social behaviour problems . . . and have significantly larger social networks than the remaining patients. When assessed at 'baseline' leavers from both hospitals were significantly more likely to express a desire to leave hospital.[18]

In order to take account of the possible bias of the results of the reprovision process reported so far, the development of one NHS hostel project targeted precisely at those otherwise likely to be left behind can be considered. The hostel opened in January 1987, housing twelve of the most disabled residents of Friern in a large semi-detached house some five miles from the hospital. Since this was in effect one of the toughest tests of a free-standing community care project its progress was evaluated by a psychologist attached to the staff, part time.

The residents were all male and ranged in age from 35 to 69, having spent on average *twenty-five years* in hospital. Ten of them were diagnosed as schizophrenic.

In December 1986 shortly before their transfer,

> only one resident was rated as showing potential for discharge, five residents were rated as having a moderate handicap, and six as having a severe handicap with respect to living skills such as self care, community skills and social activity.

Half of the residents were recorded as being verbally aggressive and one as violent.

'In short', Gundrun Knoll, the assessing psychologist, comments 'the *prospective group of residents was indeed a highly dependent and disturbed group of people who would not normally be found in a hostel in the community'.* (my emphasis)

Some preparation for the move to the community was carried out with the group over the latter part of 1986, though there is some dispute as to how structured and sustained it was. A leaving group was initiated on the ward but there was no increase among leavers in the amount of time spent on constructive activity. As part of the preparation a video was made showing the house to which the group was to move, since some patients had refused to travel to see it.

Although these were not good beginnings, the level of disturbance among the leavers did not increase. In the view of the psychologist assessing the transition to the community, the staff team did 'appear to have maintained the group's well-being across this difficult period of time'.

For the first year, the aim of preventing readmission to hospital was substantially achieved, and the hostel did not differ from the other community care projects in this regard. Two residents were readmitted for short periods, each time to stabilize medication, and each following violent incidents with knives. There was a sudden upsurge in violence during July, which coincided with a period of intense heat and high humidity. Knoll suggests that the lesson of this experience for the future is that 'it might be a good idea to take some of the residents on holiday during the summer period to decrease disturbance'.

A difference from other hostels seems to have been the residents' almost complete lack of involvement in meals, shopping, cooking, washing up, and so on. This meant that the staff had to carry out these tasks since funding for a full-time cleaner had not been included in the budget. The obvious consequence was that the hostel quickly became dirty and squalid. This led to its being characterized by later visitors as 'a house gradually being destroyed from the inside'.

Another disappointing outcome was in relation to staff–resident interactions. What one might call the 'therapeutic input' to residents tailed off over the course of the year. Knoll recorded that initially there was a 'clear shift to more resident-orientated practices' and that the amount of interaction between staff and residents increased steadily during the first year. But the nature of the interaction changed in the same period. The social distance between the two groups increased as more and more of the interactions involved administrative matters. Compared with a proportion of 21 per cent at the beginning of the assessment, at the end of the first year '80 per cent of staff–resident interactions were of an administrative nature'. There was thus a distinct lack of a sense of community. 'For instance more staff started to bring in and use their own cups. . . . Also some staff felt that there should not be a staff–resident [community] meeting, and that they did not want to eat together with residents any more.' But Knoll also suggests that apart from these negative staff attitudes, the dwindling community spirit was probably in part due to the fact that patients had lived together on the ward often by 'keeping out of each other's way'.

Knoll describes a major problem as being one of agreeing a philosophy on treatment practices. It was particularly difficult to decide within the team whether the main effort should be to prepare residents to move on, or to enable them to achieve 'maximum functioning' within the hostel. This she notes to be a well-known problem within houses and homes for mentally ill people and one perennially coming before service-providers. Since research had shown that 'projects for mentally ill people which stressed consistency, order and organisation of goals had the fewest breakdowns among residents', Knoll comments that it was not surprising that when the staff team met the deputy unit general manager in October 1987 to discuss problems, 'all agreed that the lack of clear philosophy and guidelines was the greatest problem'.

Further difficulties concerned support for staff and day care for residents. Nursing staff were not receiving regular supervision and it was not clear what the roles of the assistant director of nursing services, team leader and deputy leader were. Care plans supported by the key worker system were for the most part not implemented systematically, partly because of staff shortages. Five residents who were considered potentially able to benefit from day care had no suitable facility to go to.

In one area at least, however, the use made of local facilities, the evaluator did feel that the project was doing extremely well. Two residents were attending a local evening club, one was attending an ILEA tailoring class, one was regularly using the local library and two were church-goers. Most residents had been to the local community centre and cafés.

Interviewed at two stages during their first year, most residents expressed a preference for the hostel over Friern – seven out of twelve in April and eight in November. On each occasion three residents expressed a preference for Friern. As Knoll starkly points out, 'this leaves a few residents who have consistently said that they do not want to live at [the hostel]'. Nevertheless, no established procedure existed for reviewing their placement there.

So far in this chapter the outcome of the move to the community has been viewed first through the eyes of professional researchers. How have the community placements been perceived by lay visitors?

In June 1989 the Hampstead Community Health Council (North Camden area) produced a report on visits which a group of its members had made to three staffed group homes opened within the reprovision programme.[19] Generally they felt the homes to represent a fairly successful method of reprovision. At the same time they felt that residents lacked sufficient personal space with the houses being somewhat cramped. The group commented on one of the houses:

> It is clearly not possible or wise to pass judgement on the success or failure of the whole scheme without much greater acquaintance with individual residents and staff, but overall we were very impressed by the house. . . .
>
> There are certain major improvements on life in Friern such as comfort, more flexibility about eating and bathing arrangements, more money to spend. However . . . our ideas about privacy and dignity may not be shared by all long-stay patients. We feel that the reaction to moving from Friern will vary from person to person. For some there is a loss of space and anonymity which Friern afforded. Since most bedrooms here are double and there is no obvious quiet room to escape observation or to receive visitors the house may not suit all temperaments.
>
> One gentleman commented 'they never leave us alone'. We had the impression though that most of the residents would prefer this way of life and gain in self-esteem.[20]

Interestingly in a discussion about care plans which the group had with the nursing officer responsible for the homes, the latter said that she felt 'residents had been therapized enough', commenting that a review of each person's development was undertaken every three months with the community psychiatrist. This raises issues as to how far any 'treatment' environment is appropriate.

At another of the houses the head of the home indicated how, after two and a half years of operation, the deinstitutionalization process was 'very visible'. While at Friern, one woman resident did not go out at all, but since moving to the house she was able to go out by herself. Another woman suffering from agoraphobia did not leave the ward when living at the hospital but managed to go out into the garden at the house.

A similar picture was painted of the final one of the three houses the group of CHC members visited, where the head of the home, who had trained at Friern and had known some of the residents for more than eight years told them that

> No one will yet do chores without prompting and no one has a realistic chance at the moment of work. They have nevertheless improved 200%. In the past it would not have been possible to go shopping, prepare meals, travel to a day centre or take a bus.[21]

Despite the improvement two people wished to move on to be independent and two or three other residents were reported as finding it difficult to cope and wanting to return to hospital.

In all the houses the CHC was concerned about the high staff turnover (said to be equivalent to a number double the total staff complement for one of the houses during its first five months!) which they felt must have had an unsettling effect on residents.[22] Its members also felt that the valuable contribution made by care assistants, drawn from a variety of backgrounds, should be enhanced, and their pay and conditions decoupled from the clinical nurse grading structure. Finally the ownership and management of the houses by the health authority was considered to weaken the potential for residents to be more closely involved in the running of the houses and for their interest to be kindled in moving on.

One of the homes in which Perring was based was also internally evaluated by the voluntary organization running it. In keeping with the general outcome for people moving to the community there had not been any big changes in residents. Staff commented that

> We have not expected vast, easily measurable changes in residents. However all have, in their own ways, been active participants in decisions about programmes of development concerning the arrangements and organisation of home surroundings and needs. We have all got to know each other over the past year and have tried to guard against seeing the residents as primarily carriers of pathology or other kind of damage but rather as people first and foremost with their own habits, tastes, sense of humour and areas of particular interest.

Quite a high level of input to programmes for residents was being given in this project. For example, for an African resident speaking little English, who was reported to be very isolated in the house, one of the workers had started a programme using Lexicon cards, Scrabble letters and tapes in an effort to help him to improve his communication skills. Residents were younger than at the other hostels and group homes discussed here and therefore more active. The voluntary organization is one committed to the provision of sheltered work and day activities. It is more or less a condition of being offered a place in one of the homes which it runs that the prospective residents should be willing to attend such activities. Most residents thus continued to attend either workshops or day centres on a regular basis after their move to the community.

Generally speaking, it was reported that there had been a 'very positive response from the community' in the first two years of the project's life. The evaluators noted that

> Residents have visited pubs, cinemas, theatres, local fêtes, parks, exhibitions and jumble sales and have met on the whole only tolerance and acceptance. They have all had access to local shops, dry cleaners, newsagents, barbers and financial services without any abnormal problems.

But it was in the area of relations with local neighbours that the major problem had also occurred. Although one resident took to begging for money and cigarettes at times, and therefore drew attention to himself, the problems were due largely to the presence of a 'trouble-maker' well known to the police, who was living in the street where the project was located. Another neighbour, a freelance journalist, claimed to represent others when complaining that the house residents were not supervised adequately. The problem with the 'trouble-maker' was dealt with by consultation with solicitors, and it was decided that legal action should be taken against this person if his unpleasant threats to residents continued.

The experience of such hostility can be considered atypical of most of the projects. In several instances there were stormy public meetings prior to their opening, but after they had been established, in general, few problems with neighbours were reported. This perhaps reflected the weak integration of hospital 'leavers' with the surrounding community that Perring's analysis highlights.

Conclusion

It is clear that the outcome did bestow many benefits on the people who moved in the early years of reprovision. These centred upon the lifting of restrictions summarized in Godin's concepts of positive and negative freedom. Equally clearly, the move out of hospital did not in itself 'cure' mental illness or lead to the leavers being unambigously satisfied with the placement. It is significant that half of the TAPS sample of 117 leavers did not state positively that they wished to stay in the new accommodation, given that they were being interviewed by psychiatrists and psychologists whose professional background made them not entirely independent of the medical and paramedical establishments. It is quite possible that a greater proportion of those resettled might reveal themselves as harbouring a desire for an alternative, if advised independently about the options that might be made available by people not attached in any way to the discipline of medicine. Some elements of the 'benign' authority of hospitals are evident in the group homes. At the same time these homes, paradoxically given their community setting, are seen by some residents as affording less of an opportunity to meet people than the large institution, and as making it more difficult to get away from others, thus heightening tensions between house occupants. Taking what would certainly be an over-critical stance, one could argue that the establishment of the 'purpose-planned group homes' represented nothing more than an extension of hospital half-way houses reaching out from the asylums into residential communities. By looking in this harsh light at what is an undoubtedly positive change, attention can be turned back toward the unfulfilled promise of the planning process. By resettling long-stay hospital residents it was intended to provide a new deal for all the mentally ill. But the new health centres, the accessible 'walk-in' refuges, the new forms of domiciliary care, the new work opportunities, and the new leisure activities were barely in evidence. Why?

References

1 Dated Trinity Sunday 1983 from the Reverend Victor A. Stock of the Parish Church of St James the Great and the Church of St John the Evangelist.
2 Perring, C.A. (1990). Leaving the hospital behind? An anthropological study of group homes in two London boroughs. Unpublished PhD thesis, London School of Economics.
3 ibid., p. 255.
4 Godin, P. (1990). The Fencepiece Road Project, *Senior Nurse* 10, 3: 7–13.
5 Team for the Assessment of Psychiatric Services (1988). *Preliminary Report on Baseline Data for Friern and Claybury Hospitals*, London, North East Thames Regional Health Authority.
6 Team for the Assessment of Psychiatric Services (1990). *Moving Long Stay Psychiatric Patients into the Community: First Results. TAPS Fourth Annual Conference*, London, North East Thames Regional Health Authority, p. 49.
7 Dayson, D. and Gooch, C. (1990). Clinical and Social Outcomes of the Long Term Mentally Ill After One Year in the Community: Results from the First Three Cohorts, in TAPS, *Better Out Than In?* Report from the 5th Annual Conference. London, North East Thames Regional Health Authority.
8 Wills, W., Dayson, D. and Gooch, C. (1990). Patients' Attitudes Before and After Discharge, in TAPS, *Better Out Than In?* Report from the 5th Annual Conference. London, North East Thames Regional Health Authority, p. 6.
9 Wills, Dayson and Gooch (1990), p. 3.
10 Godin (undated), p. 13.
11 ibid., p. 13.
12 Perring (1990), p. 7.
13 ibid., p. 7.
14 ibid., p. 99.
15 ibid., p. 133.
16 ibid., p. 160.
17 ibid., pp. 163–4.
18 Jones, D. (1989). The selection of patients for reprovision, in Team for the Assessment of Psychiatric Patients, *Moving Long Stay Patients into the Community: First Results*, London, NETRHA.
19 Hampstead Community Health Council (1989). *A Report of Community Health Council Visits to Three Houses Opened by Hampstead Health Authority as Part of the Friern Closure Programme*, June, London, Hampstead CHC.
20 ibid., p. 4.
21 ibid., p. 10.
22 ibid., p. 11.

7

Conclusion

Judged as an administrative reform, the process of reproviding mental hospitals described in this book has clearly resulted in a laudable transfer of care. Residents have experienced a sense of liberation as restrictions have been lifted and their living conditions improved. However, the vision that had stimulated the reform was one of a much wider panorama than that of a transfer of care. In devising the framework for the closure of its mental hospitals, the NETRHA presented an opportunity to the health authorities in the catchment areas of Friern and Claybury. For the first time since the nineteenth century a major funded initiative for the development of completely new local services was in prospect. The question was, would district health authorities, which were still organizational novices in 1983, be sensitive enough to local public needs, be they cultural, age-specific, or socio-demographic, to develop projects which could be owned and valued by local communities? The reforms which would place the technical–professional assessment of need as the highest order of DHA activity were still eight years away. But the NETRHA gave its constituent districts a fairly free hand to design new services. In some ways, this placed unwelcome responsibilities on DHAs. Reprovision entailed a fundamental planning dilemma. Was it to be new care homes for the old one or was it to be a new care deal? Could or should the slate be wiped clean and new arrangements be based on canvassing the views of informed and concerned local publics?

As Friern and Claybury events unfolded, the athenian utopia in which consumer and purchaser choice would determine what kind of services were to be provided, began to take on legislative forms. Decentralization, as a means of involving consumers organizations in decision and provision by the state, began to assume a dated and unfashionable appearance. As was noted in Chapter 3, the Athenian model of authority, by contrast, arguably became more relevant to discussions about public choice. While DHAs were

henceforward to purchase care on behalf of their population, a cardinal principle of the purchases was to be the satisfaction of consumer requirements.
Consumers, of course, differ in the extent to which they are sufficiently
informed and motivated to make demands for services. As long as DHAs are
intermediaries between the public and the provider hospitals, and the athenian utopia remains for this reason elusive, they will need to assume that
their population possesses the civic skills to represent its interests. At the
same time, it is broadly accepted that some groups will require advocates to
make their needs known to DHA surveillance. DHAs thus remain intrac-
tably involved in issues of civic competence.

To turn reprovision toward the development of new care deals for the
public, health authorities would have probably had to adopt a decentralized or an Athenian mode of planning. As the cases of Haringey and
Waltham Forest show, the market of agencies in the mental health field
was often too weak to support the model of operation of an autarchic
authority. However, decentralized or athenian authority action would require that the vocational ownership of the mentally ill by the professional
carers, however benevolent its patriarchal intent, would have to be surren-
dered. Users and carers' groups, ethnic minority groups and neighbourhood
associations would all have had to be admitted to the court of decision-
making. Islington was the one authority which inhabited an environment
allowing an autarchic model for its planning decisions, which were framed
within limits of professional judgement, political trust and moral obligation. It was bold enough to both fund a Users Group and admit it to one of
the planning forums. However, the DHA was not prepared to consider the
shared planning and implementation proposals from the voluntary sector.
Waltham Forest did not take the opportunity to create a district specific
service. Very clearly, as a move to first base towards a service which might
still change in the future, new care homes for the old one were to be
created. In Haringey, where the large ethnic minority presence cried out for
a DHA venture into Community Development for mental health, the
Authority was, unfortunately, ill-suited as a corporate planning agency to
undertake such work.

The planning problem was certainly picked up in each area at an early
stage. It was identified as an issue of settling the priority between two sets
of need. First, the elderly inpatient population required resettlement. Second, the putative needs, insofar as they were predictable, of that proportion
of the population of Haringey which was likely to fall victim to mental
illness in the future had to be met. This was interpreted as an issue for
medical and nursing staff. On the basis of their views, hospital residents
were commonly judged to need the levels of continuous *residential* support which only staffed homes and hostels could provide. Some could of
course be later weaned off such support. But the majority would need
support in this type of shelter for the rest of their lives.

A striking feature of the planning process was the faith placed in

professional assessment of the dependency levels of the inpatient population, with individual needs for supervision being 'read off' according to
the lack of dressing, cooking, socializing skills and so on. Despite research
at another North East Thames psychiatric hospital indicating that many
long-stay patients could make an informed decision about the type of
placements that might be available to them, client choices played a very
small part in the development work.[1] Now that DHAs and SSDs are to
determine community need, the likelihood of any alternative conceptual-
izations of such need put forward by voluntary organizations, users groups,
or housing associations being marginalized, as happened in the Friern and
Claybury process, is all the more apparent.

If there had been more input into a process of informing patients about
the options, from an early stage, the planning dilemma might have been
resolved. For, as the Dayson and Wills research discussed in Chapter 6
indicates, once resettled, a good proportion of those who had moved out of
Friern and Claybury wanted to move to a place of their own.

What is surprising is the way in which the two types of care – residential
for the old, non-residential for the new – were polar opposites within
professional imagery. Group homes were not, in themselves, incompatible
with forms of supervised placement allowing more autonomy in domestic
living arrangements. As Thornicroft noted in a review of their function in
the Fulbourn Hospital catchment area as long ago as 1979, group homes
could be houses divided up into single bedsits, or they could be homes in
which kitchen and bath were shared between all residents.[2] It was thus odd
that it was not until the later stages of reprovision, following housing
association advice, as much as health authority rethinking, that 'cluster'
bedsits were proposed as a form of provision which *would* be suitable for
highly dependent hospital residents. Even then, the judgement of professional carers was still the basis for change, the theory being that the bedsit
arrangement would allow the more individualistic, antisocial or mercurial
a little more living space.

It is not difficult for readers conversant with the literature to think of
'back-of-envelope' solutions to the planning dilemma. For example instead
of having two seven-place staffed group homes, an authority could have
struck up a deal with a housing association or trust to secure nomination
rights to a range of its accommodation. Client choice and professional
systems of support might indicate that a mix of, say, three two-bedroomed
sharers' flats, four single-person flats and four bedsits – distributed reasonably evenly in the property of the association – would be the optimum
portfolio of contracted units. Since associations are 'zoned' by the housing
corporation, it is likely that the property would all be located in one neighbourhood. The DHA's flats and bedsits could then be supervised by neighbourhood care teams, perhaps made up of four whole-time staff each shift,
working in pairs. Clearly some residents would need the briefest visit or
phone-call daily to check that they had set about the daily routine of

getting out of bed, washing and dressing. Others would require, perhaps, in problematic cases forty-five minutes of help with washing, and others might need the back-up of the resource team, or community psychiatric nurses if the support workers sensed the client was becoming more troubled. In return for nomination rights to its property, the host association would have to be offered something by the DHA, such as land or a one-off cash amount of capital.

Such suggestions as this brings a whole company of difficulties with them. Apart from the goodwill of housing association members and tenants which would be required, given their already active role in deinstitutionalization, health authorities would need the flexibility to make the offers of land or capital to them. DHAs have not acted as housing authorities on any scale, and are unlikely to have the staff to assess market conditions and options along these lines. NHS capital assets had, of course, been a 'free good', until the 1990 legislation.

It is not only because of the desire for greater independence among residents that group homes might be allotted a lesser place in the planning system. Some long-term hospital residents might well express a preference for a care situation in which they are cooked for and have their clothes washed for them. Elderly men may not want to participate in the domestic chores which group homes entail. If care homes give sufficient freedom within a residential area while offering 'laid-on' meals, drinks and medical care, then reproviding of this kind is not necessarily rendered dubious on the ground of commercial gain. For those residents needing simply 'prodding' from care workers to occupy themselves, community nurses could be attached to residential care homes for elderly people or non-mental health specific hostels, which are able to accommodate those hospital residents who express an informed preference for shelter of that kind. Indeed this is no more than to suggest a time-honoured means of resettlement. It would leave more resources from closures for day care and activity, subjects which I consider below.

Whatever the feasibility of such solutions their key feature would be that the team of caring professionals would not live in with residents, though they would be an intercom alarm call or telephone call away within the neighbourhood. With the inevitable reduction through deaths of the elderly clients who had made up the majority of long-stay hospital residents, the neighbourhood team would be able to take on new entrants to the service from within their catchment area. Such clients referred for long-term support would be living in a range of accommodation, perhaps 'with family' or in personally owned/tenanted flats and houses.

With the emphasis of legislation in the 1990s very much on the role of the private and voluntary sectors, the onus has moved even further than before towards housing associations to take centre place as housing authorities. Their role has been very minor compared with that of the 'Habitations Loyer à Modéré' (HLMs), the semi-public housing societies of France, which provide most of the country's social housing. With the 1991 approach to capital assets in the NHS requiring that they be costed as a daily charge to health care purchasers, trusts and the reformed DHAs are now, in theory, in a much better position to pursue trade-offs of land or property with associations which can offer housing nomination rights. The development of consortia between DHAs and housing associations, which also involve the other major care-giving agencies, though still a process in its infancy, as in Haringey, does offer a much greater level of housing expertise for the task.

Affordable single person's housing is an extremely scarce resource in Britain. Trends are similar to those in the USA where home ownership has reached an almost identical peak as it has in Britain (65 per cent as compared to 64 per cent of households). Because of a huge increase in house prices in the USA (from a median price of $69,300 in 1982 for a single family home to a median of $120,000 in 1990) home ownership among young people has begun to drop significantly.[3] It is thus likely that this trend will also become apparent in Britain. Dreier and Atlas report that many low-income holders of 'housing allowances' in the USA cannot find apartments to rent, because they are outbid for those available by people not dependent on allowances. The American housing crisis has brought with it a descent of middle-income people down from home ownership to renting. There has therefore been a squeeze in the rented sector on low-income households finding themselves having to fight hard for space within it. This has dramatic consequences for people who have a history of mental illness and who wish for their 'own place', since they are unlikely, after any period in hospital, to have the income or resources to fund the high levels of mortgage payments which are the market alternative.

> The initial stereotype of the homeless person was of an alcoholic or mentally ill middle aged man or 'bag lady' – many of them victims of the deinstitutionalisation policies that began in the 1970s. But by the mid-1980s, the composition of the homeless population began to change. Studies by the US Conference of Mayors (UCSM) and others have found an increasing number of entire families among the homeless including many young children. The latest UCSM survey found that almost one quarter of the homeless *work* but simply have wages too low to afford permanent housing.[4]

Dreier and Atlas see signs of hope that housing has increased in salience as a political issue in the USA. More housing Bills were filed in Congress in 1988 than in any other year of the decade. Not-for-Profit organizations, which are often religious foundations, have supported the rebuilding of housing for shared equity or 'fair rents' in rundown city areas. Community pressure has also achieved legislation which obliges lenders to meet the 'community credit' needs of all neighbourhoods. Dreier and Atlas suggest that this legislation be strengthend so that the financial institutions have to provide low interest loans for affordable housing and to lend to community development agencies.

Wilmott and Murie argue that Britain can learn from France in addressing its housing shortage.[5] This could be done first through protection and enhancement of public housing, and second through the strengthening of the semi-public housing societies. The HLMs in France act as major developers and managers of 'moderate rent' housing. Some HLMs were set up by big companies or nationalized industries, such as Renault and the Paris Regional Transport Authority, to provide accommodation for their employees. Others were founded by chambers of commerce, religious and voluntary organizations. The loans which support the activity are subsidized by central government, with additional funding coming from a 'pay-roll' tax levied by local authorities on firms with more than ten employees.

Home ownership has grown in France in a like manner to its growth in Britain. The phenomenon is therefore not simply due to political radicalism. Wilmott and Murie argue that the 'new diversity' in social housing should be recognized as established. Housing associations and trusts should be largely removed from government control in order to ease their work in providing it. Social housing could then be achieved through government-supported commercial loans for 'fair rent' lettings or shared ownership schemes. Local authorities should, in Wilmot and Murie's view, 'keep a watching brief over this activity, and have the powers to ensure that the proportions of different kinds of social housing are reasonable to meet the district's needs, stepping in as necessary to encourage or directly promote new schemes.'[6]

These American and European housing trends suggest that legislation or guidance which imposes similar obligations on big British lenders to those imposed on financial institutions on the two continents, if supported by Government subsidy, could make a significant impact on the shortage of affordable housing. With local authorities ensuring the provision of a range of low-income housing, mentally ill people would have some protection. But in addition the consortia of mental health agencies would seek a major involvement in community credit packages.

If some of the funds extracted from the closing of mental hospitals are to be put into housing for mentally ill people, then the prospects for housing provision suggest that a significant proportion of single-person apartments should be provided. The Housing Act 1989 gives clear indication that the municipal housing sector will continue to shrink, and it is in this sector primarily that low-cost single-person accommodation can be obtained. DHAs will have little choice but to look to associations, trusts and societies to secure access to a range of housing for the shelter of their long-term dependants. At the same time the apparent willingness of the Church, in its *Faith in the City* initiative to use its lands for social housing, indicates that there are charitable resources in that sector to be brought into play in favour of mentally ill people.[7]

Was the apparent failure to solve the planning problem and provide for the two distinct types of need in the new service due to lack of resources to do the job properly? Was the task of balancing the needs within hospital budgets which were long claimed to be substantially underfunded, simply unrealistic – since they presumed that a transition from one low institutional cost base to another low community cost base could be achieved? It could be argued that local state planners, devoid of a sufficient degree of civic competence among members of the public on the one hand and any Athenian approach to planning from within their own authorities on the other, would have great difficulty in grasping the opportunities created by the closure initiative. But planners themselves argued that the resources were not there to carry out both tasks – the construction of the new alternatives for future clients, and the retirement of the asylum populations to the community.

Few planning solutions to the Friern and Claybury task were acclaimed. But many won approval and they could, to a certain extent, have created some elements of new types of service within the overall reprovision. CMHCs were retained in plans, even if their role was not taken up with enthusiasm and their potential contribution appears to have often been seen as somewhat marginal. It was recognized that it was important to reprovide the social life function of Friern and Claybury, and the need to do this tied in well with the need to support the few evening clubs and drop-in centres established in the catchment area.

Organizational problems dogged the planning process but far more important than any accusation of failure or cost-cutting was one fundamental restriction on 'action space' for authorities. Hospital beds for acute admissions and the new long-stay population, supported by day hospitals, all to be run by the NHS, were more or less axiomatic to any health authority plan. At the same time, the task of resettlement was undeniably one involving at least some expensive supported housing, whatever model of service delivery was chosen. There were supporters of the original American model of change, in which it had been intended that CMHCs would play a central role, their work spanning the range from provision of inpatient services to provision of consultation and education. Those who were enthusiastic about such a programme, especially where working in areas with minimal community services, saw the move from Friern and Claybury hospitals as a chance to do away with a significant number of the normative requirement of acute beds. But in the end, partly because of the power of symbolic normative values and partly because experimenting with alternatives meant major disruption to professional roles, the enthusiasts for change were a powerless minority.

At its heart, deinstitutionalization has a central concern with *individual* rights. Packages of care are 'tailored' to individual needs, thus bringing about an end to any kind of mass provision of care. The NHS takes responsibility for patients with highly differentiated treatment needs rather than mentally ill people as a unitary group. The intent of the NHS and Community Care Bill is that this differentiation be carried through sufficiently to recognize the validity of differences between the needs for care of individuals. It is thus designed to overcome the traditional lumping together of these needs to suit the organization of welfare bureaux into large client based departments, such as those serving the elderly population. The types of package of care are in theory unlimited, in line with the ideology that individual needs should not be aggregated because this would lead to the provision of an insensitive form of service delivery. But where packages of care are disaggregated as, for instance, from the standardized shelter and care offered by the asylum, recipients are essentially alone. In hospital, the very act of standardization lumped them together in such a way that they might be able to recognize their common needs. The converse of the principle of individual care is the lack of a community of recipients. Opportunities for collective action and empowerment are therefore fewer in the community setting.

This 'downside' to the resettlement process in which patients become to a certain extent scattered among poor or unemployed people and other marginal social groups has implications for professional carers, too. Their major concern is the prospect of a rapid dilution of care and resources, as needs specific to the client group become, in theory, a thing of the past.

The aloneness in the community of a significant proportion of service recipients, and their relative lack of opportunity for giving and receiving mutual support, militates against collective action for employment. Such action is clearly important where jobs are subject to strong competition, and, as disadvantaged individuals, those who have suffered mental illness are often considered too risky to employ.

It has been argued by Visser and Wijnhoven that unemployment has been accepted by European electorates, as a natural fact of the economic environment of the late twentieth century and that alternative strategies for full employment from the political Centre and Left have been rejected. They draw this inference from a study of electoral outcomes of the last decade in which conservative parties performed well and were not 'punished' for mass unemployment.[8]

If mass unemployment has become accepted then it opens up the depressing American vista of the future for the disabled person as someone 'who gets a pension and can use his time well at home' but who, as one of the 'vocationally disabled' is likely to be 'condemned and isolated, rather than integrated into a community and liberated from drudgery'.[9]

Set in this context, the Italian experience discussed in Chapter 1 is most relevant for the future of those discharged from asylums. The fact that the patients' co-operative formed at the Trieste Mental Hospital won the contract for cleaning within it indicates that contracts tendered for by client or resident organizations in the community are winnable with sympathetic employers. Employment prospects for people leaving hospital as individuals with packages of care are not likely to improve. But they may be strengthened in organizations which are large enough to negotiate with employers, to lobby, to fund development workers from contract funding, and to multiply themselves in different geographical areas.

The evolution of such co-operatives is not of course antithetical to state or charitable support for a nation-wide campaign to ensure that the existing legislation which supports the position of disabled people, and places duties in regard to their employment on employers, is enforced.

While work has been seen as intrinsic to rehabilitation of mentally ill people, several forces can be noted which devalue work for the population at large. The routinization of tasks in industrial production makes for its intrinsic unattractiveness for prospective employees. The remoteness of many work tasks from the production and consumption of goods which are of value in the worker's domestic world, entails a loss of the individual's identification with his or her work. As Cohen suggests:

> On the one hand, work is considered to be a royal road to self-actualization and is exemplified by creative work. On the other hand, work is seen as a resented requirement of living in a civilized world and is exemplified by work on the assembly line.[10]

In the discussion of Christel Lane's work on marginal employment in Chapter 1, it was noted that while part-timers may have opted for part-time work, their rights are in fact less than those of full-time workers, and thus they are in this sense exploited. There is a danger that people who have mental illness histories, and who join the marginal employed groups will be subject to the same sort of manipulation as characterized the 'institutional peonage' that had been left behind in the large hospitals: hence the importance of collective strength. A key role of agencies etablished by and for patients or community residents would be to contract for types of work which were sufficiently varied to constitute reasonably attractive employment. For the tradition of the Christmas cracker factory dies hard. Sadly, there is a drift downward to casual jobs of the kitchen portering type among psychiatric patients which has to be reversed. A degree of autonomy over work won by the workers' agency is the means of assuring that more complex tasks are organized both to fulfil personal capacities and not to tax individuals unduly, depending on the needs and abilities of the people who are members.

Many social policy analysts have argued for the devotion of a greater proportion of municipal funding to the support of mentally ill people. In the 1990 legislation, the duty of assessment of community care needs imposed upon local authorities, and the provision of specific grants for resettlement of patients from the large hospitals, both augur well.

However, it is highly unlikely that in the mixed economy of welfare so vigorously pursued, any significant increase would be achieved in the funding specifically devoted to those with a history of mental illness or those in the community requiring support.

In Chapter 1 the lack of any popular sentiment for improving the lot of mentally ill people was discussed. While the welfare state is, in Atherton's phrase, 'still on solid ground' in that the public remains committed to supporting the poor and destitute, it is not gaining ground.[11] Disabled and poor people are not, it seems, to be pulled out of their marginal existence.

Without a commitment to a relative improvement in the social position of disabled people, the principles of normalization cannot apply. This is because the aim of normalization is to give a more-than-equal chance of participation in civil and economic life to the disadvantaged person. The realization of this aim naturally depends upon the majority social groups accepting a corresponding reduction in their own social status. For the elderly residents moving out of the hospitals and back into the community, the problem is not so apparent: as is clear from the case of Friern and Claybury, few will be expected to work on the open market, and few will be competing for independent housing, given the 'group home' dominated structure of reprovision. As Perring's work indicates, only a very modest demand for integration is in fact being placed on localities. For the next generation of mentally ill people, the case is different again, for here the housing and employment contest will be on. Indeed it is a central aim of professional care workers with whom the new mentally ill will have contact to support their clients in 'maintaining face' in the community, whether in their neighbourhood, at work or in leisure activities. This indicates that the idea of local care having the effect of normalizing the person is being confused with normalization itself. In fact the latter process, where stringently followed, poses a threat to the social order of localities.

The outcome within the Friern and Claybury process at the hostel for some of the most dependent patients indicated that conversation and other social skills are not likely to be quickly rediscovered in the transition to the community. At the other projects there was no greater evidence of more friendships being kept up outside hospital than in it. This lack of change raises a number of issues about what may be expected of social interaction in urban communities. For many people, social contact in the local community may be inherently unfulfilling. But aside from social interaction beyond its confines, opportunites for fulfilment from vicarious participation in the fictitious localities portrayed in the media are clearly important. Thus Hobson comments that

Television is very important to the elderly and housebound and while the rest of society fails to alleviate the situation for many elderly people who live alone, the entertainment and sense of contact which programmes like *Crossroads* provide for its viewers are surely among the most valuable aspects of the medium . . . *the reassurances which they derive from fictional programmes should not be under-estimated.*[12] (my emphasis)

Taylor and Mullan, who cite Hobson's view in their book *Uninvited Guests*, commissioned research with a cross-section of television audiences. They asked viewers the question

What kind of person is your television set – male? female? warm? cold? a friend? a critic?

They found that the most usual description of the television set was as a friend, with companionship or company the most notable feature of its personhood. For elderly people there was evidence that it fulfilled even greater 'social' needs, perhaps being 'something without which life became very difficult'.

EVA (72): I was going to say that I'm in all day and it's company for me.
ETHEL (79): I've got a nerve condition and I've got to have something in the house.
EVA: It's a friend to a lot of people.
ETHEL: I can't be on my own indoors, otherwise I've got to have the doors and windows open. But if the television's on it's all right.
ALICE (77): It's psychological.
ROSE (74): I used to know a lady, and when anyone had a drink on the television she'd go and get herself one and drink with them. (*All laugh*) If he's going to have one, I'll have one with him.[13]

Taylor and Mullan found that British 'Soaps' were likely to evoke 'particularly strong identification'. They comment that at the heart of this identification

seems to lie the fact of 'carrying on', of 'coping'. What most moves viewers to tears is the sight of a stoical character, one who has endured all the sufferings of hardship which can be unleashed upon them by a diligent scriptwriter, finally giving in.
JOY (27): It was so very sad when you saw it, the funeral, and then her, Hilda (from *Coronation Street*), who'd been so strong through all of it. And then when her son went, and she unwrapped the parcel, didn't she, with his clothes? She broke down. At the sight of the clothes. In the end it was too much for her.[14]

Are the eternal questions about community and association raised within sociology so important? Does community depend on proximity of dwellings and communal work arrangements within a locality, as Tönnies believed?[15] It is certainly difficult entirely to sustain the thesis that community is an ideological tool of the state for maintaining social solidarity. If, as Hobson suggests, television communities enable viewers to have a sense of contact which society fails to give them, then dissatisfaction with or at least ambivalence towards local community would appear to be the norm.[16]

This discussion of the way in which community is, in part, a product of the imagination, has clear implications for resettlement of residents of institutions. For integration, perhaps too much importance is attached to residents being conjoined to the community by active participation in festivals and fêtes, church services and community centre activities. While a wider variety of pursuits is on offer than those available in large hospitals, participation in them, like neighbouring, may also carry social obligations that are difficult to fulfil.[17] A television community does not carry any such demands. Judging from the early results of the Friern and Claybury study, staff of group homes may have to continue to initiate group activities and to prompt the participants to see them through.

A suggestion that residents should have a choice between vicarious participation in community activities, and those which staff encourage them to be involved in within the local areas, would gain the person who made it little credibility. This is a complex issue. Elderly people may ordinarily expect to have the dignified leisure of retirement, a period in which they 'come to terms with life-events'. Where one person's laziness can constitute resistance to rehabilitation efforts, another's can be taken as evidence of a successfully pursued coping strategy.

Focusing on attitudes towards television is not to suggest that it has the franchise on a sense of belonging that the local community does not. Neither is it to suggest that the creation of such a sense of belonging for chronic mentally ill people should be left to the power of the imagination of each of them. But it is to suggest that the role of the local community is limited, especially given that its development is often dependent on the actions of multinational companies or central government rather than local actors. Since kinship networks are dispersed well beyond local areas of residence, and employment for many is also at locations which are quite distant from their homes, the issues of integration and belonging do not equate to those of community, locality and neighbourhood. And breaking into neighbouring is a tricky process for anyone moving into a new area.

Moreover the romance of local togetherness, and its images of family warmth and accepting communities, where friends are made at clubs and over garden walls, distracts attention from the key issue for future services, civic autonomy in planning, management and monitoring. Such autonomy can be achieved only through policies of community development. While carers' and users' groups provide an initial focus for such work, wider public interest groups, such as the Black Health Workers' and Patients' Group, which responded to the Haringey mental health strategy discussed in Chapter 5, are clearly ready to be engaged.

From the case studies reported here, little 'community' intervention and shaping of policies for the new non-institutional services for mentally ill people took place. To the extent that health issues were salient for the public they ranged around local concern for the future of general hospitals. It was rare indeed for any large gathering to be organized to press the case for mental health service developments. The public was aroused in a hostile way periodically when the planting of long-stay residents in their community was perceived as a threat.

Strategies for civic autonomy in the development of mental health services could learn from the community development projects of the 1970s which central government supported.[18] Some input of funding would be required. The funding would have to be channelled through local government since the initiatives would have to be sustained long-term rather than being marooned in one-off 'outposted' and 'time-limited' ministerial experiments. As with the Griffiths community care reforms this would run against the shift of the locus of control of welfare from the town halls to central government. It would also not be entirely in tune with the idea of shifting power away from providers in local welfare departments to the receivers of services. But to say this is merely to recognize an intrinsic contradiction in the efforts of local councils to devolve powers over public affairs to neighbourhoods and residential localities. This is that local states have to set up and control the mechanisms for allowing the discretion in public decision-making to happen.

If central government is not in favour of funding municipal programmes for facilitating civic autonomy, then the private and voluntary sector becomes the heir presumptive to consumer/community development. Many voluntary organizations depend heavily on statutory sector funding and in the private sector social security benefits, still controlled by the central state, play an equally large part. The case for the private and voluntary sector to represent consumer interests independently is thus not always credible.

A more practical alternative might be for community development work to be laid down as a mental health care purchasers' contract condition. Croft and Beresford suggest principles upon which social services departments should base community participation.[19] These could as easily be adopted by DHAs or their equivalents. They include

1 key people, groups or bodies inside the agency to be dedicated to the initiative and carrying it forward
2 placing emphasis on user involvement in recruitment, training and promotion
3 funding being conditional on people's involvement
4 earmarked budgets to increase people's say and involvement
5 more participatory management systems
6 continuous monitoring and evaluation.

The importance of community development in service change cannot be over-emphasized, for without it the facilities within the community will be as distant from people as the asylum was. The barriers imposed by professional and technical decision-making will be as much of an impediment to services being locally meaningful as was geographical distance between catchment area and the hospital on the hill.

The theme of civic participation in community care is a fitting one with which to conclude this book, for it offers the hope of autonomy for people who have, traditionally, had things done to them, as captives of willing patrons. The diversity of views among the patrons about forms of service which would ensure the 'best outcome' for patients is clearly so great that professional and technical judgement, however well intentioned, cannot be relied upon to produce, *de facto*, the most responsible form of future service. The irony of the 1991 health and welfare reforms is that the power of this judgement has been strengthened, apparently in contradiction of the trend away from decision and provision by the state. At the same time, the cult of localism has been such a fair wind behind the athenian utopia that the empirical truths of localities, the unevenness and vulnerability of entrepreneurial voluntary and informal sector initiatives, have been over-looked. If the athenian utopia is to have any meaning for the local state, then it is required to involve users and carers in decision-making, together with those in local communities who have an interest. The British appear neither Swiss-like nor Italian-like in their commitment to community action. Thus it is incumbent on the state to create the conditions for civic autonomy and to design feasible equivalents for local standing conventions on health issues. The kind of initiatives which Croft and Beresford propose provide a basis for such work. Then, at least popular choices between the options can be made. While legislative or administrative restraints must be applied to guard against the possibility of local community malice toward, and marginalization of, mentally ill people, the scope for developing services sensitive to local cultures is immense.

References

1 Abrahamson, D. and Brenner, D. (1982). Do long stay patients want to leave hospital?, *Health Trends* 14: 95–9.
2 Thornicroft, G. (1979). Group Homes – a success?, *Nursing Times*, 11 January: 84–5.
3 Dreier, P. and Atlas, J. (1989). Grassroots strategies for the housing crisis: a national agenda, *Social Policy* Winter: 25–38.
4 ibid.: 29.
5 Wilmott, P. and Murie, A. (1988). *Polarisation and Social Housing*, London, Policy Studies Institute.
6 ibid., p. 88.

7 Report of the Archbishop of Canterbury's Commission on Urban Priority Areas (1985). *Faith in the City: A Call for Action by Church and Nation*, London, Christian Action, p. 19.
8 Visser, W. and Wijnhoven, R. (1990). Politics do matter, but does unemployment?, *European Journal of Political Research* 189: 71–96.
9 Cohen, L.J. (1990). Work and mental health: personal, social and economic contexts, *Social Psychiatry and Psychiatric Epidemiology* 25: 111.
10 ibid., p. 110.
11 Atherton, C.R. (1989). The Welfare State: still on solid ground, *Social Service Review* June: 167–79.
12 Hobson, D. (1982). *Crossroads: the Drama of a Soap Opera*, London, Methuen, quoted in L. Taylor and B. Mullan (1986). *Uninvited Guests*, London, Chatto & Windus, p. 46.
13 Taylor and Mullan (1986), p. 184.
14 ibid., pp. 45–6.
15 Tonnies, F. (1957). *Community and Association*, New York, Harper & Row.
16 Hobson (1982).
17 Robinson, F. and Abrams, P. (1977). *What We Know about the Neighbours*, Durham, University of Durham, Rowntree Research Unit.
18 Thomas, D.N. (1983). *The Making of Community Work*, London, Allen & Unwin.
19 Croft, S. and Beresford, P. (1990). *From Paternalism to Participation: Involving People in Social Services*, London, Open Service Project, p. 22.

Figure 6 The study at a glance

- Asylum closures were not initiated as a central government policy for achieving cost containment.
- The political and administrative origins of closure were diffuse. They included:
    priority policies to improve the position of marginalized and deprived social groups;
    the targeting of resources on client groups traditionally neglected;
    the pursuit of geographical equity in the NHS and of autarchic district services.
- Interim results from analysis of the resettlement process suggest that hospital leavers were generally satisfied with their community placements.
- DHA decision-making was responsive to local public pressure to a limited degree when voluntary organizations, local authorities and CHCs possessed effective lobbying skills.

But

- The underlying planning problem of how to deploy 'reprovision' resources to meet the needs **both** of hospital residents **and** of other non-hospital groups remains.
- Hospital practices and philosophies tend to have been carried over into community care services. Professional carers still consider that they have a moral obligation to provide 24-hour supervision in asylum-like facilities, primarily staffed group homes, hostels and nursing homes.
- Hospital residents were offered little choice in the types of community accommodation and activities made available.
- Although **consulted**, users' groups, carers' groups and the informed public were not involved in **making decisions** about the pattern of hospital re-placement services.
- There was a lack of engagement with social policy changes affecting mental health, such as the increase in private owner occupation as a form of housing tenure, and the increase in the part-time workforce.
- Differences in the technical capacities of DHAs to achieve the scale of planning necessary for reprovision and the administrative devolution necessary to involve community interests were not acknowledged.
- There was a shortage of 'product champions' to 'market' a range of alternatives to hospital

In conclusion

The underlying planning problem is not intractable.

- Some hospital leavers do wish to live in independent accommodation and can benefit from the same support and advisory services in employment, recreation and for citizen's rights as the non-hospital groups.
- DHAs can facilitate collective organizations by users for example in employment co-operatives.
- It is important to build on the knowledge of local groups and networks which Local Authority Community Workers have in order to involve consumers and the informed public in shaping development of care services.

Index

DATE DUE			